KAIFIYAT

KAIFIYAT

verses on love and women

KAIFI AZMI

Translated by
RAKHSHANDA JALIL

PENGUIN
VIKING
An imprint of Penguin Random House

VIKING

USA | Canada | UK | Ireland | Australia
New Zealand | India | South Africa | China | Singapore

Viking is part of the Penguin Random House group of companies
whose addresses can be found at global.penguinrandomhouse.com

Published by Penguin Random House India Pvt. Ltd
4th Floor, Capital Tower 1, MG Road,
Gurugram 122 002, Haryana, India

Penguin
Random House
India

First published in Viking by Penguin Random House India 2019

10 9 8 7 6 5 4 3 2 1

ISBN 9780670092109

Typeset in RequiemText by Manipal Digital Systems, Manipal
Printed at Replika Press Pvt. Ltd, India

www.penguin.co.in

This is a legitimate digitally printed version of the book and therefore might not
have certain extra finishing on the cover.

Translator's Dedication

To Shabana Azmi and Javed Akhtar ... who carry the legacy forward

Contents

Foreword

For Abba with Love

Early 1990s

He was always different, a fact that didn't sit too easily on my young shoulders. He didn't go to 'office' or wear the normal trousers and shirt like other 'respectable' fathers but chose to wear a white cotton kurta-pyjama twenty-four hours of the day. He did not speak English and, worse still, I didn't call him 'Daddy' like other children, but some strange-sounding 'Abba'! I learned very quickly to avoid referring to him in front of my classmates and lied that he did some vague 'business'! Imagine letting my school friends know that he was a poet. What on earth did that mean—a euphemism for someone who did no work?

Being my parent's child was, for me, unconventional in every way. My school required that both parents speak English. Since neither Abba nor Mummy did, I faked my entry into school. Sultana Jafri, Sardar Jafri's wife, pretended to be my mother and Munish Narayan Saxena, a friend of Abba's, pretended to be my father. Once in the tenth standard, the vice principal called me and said that she'd heard my father at a recent mushaira and he looked quite different from the gentleman who had come in the morning for Parents' Day! Understandably, I went completely blue in the face and said: 'Oh he's been suffering from typhoid and has lost a lot of weight, you know' . . . and made up some sort of story to save my skin!

It was no longer possible to keep Abba in the closet. He had started writing lyrics for films and one day a friend of mine said that her father had read my father's name in the newspaper. That did it! I owned him up at once! Of all the forty children in my class, only my father's name had appeared in the newspaper! I perceived his being 'different' as a virtue for the first time. I need no longer feel apologetic about his wearing a kurta-pyjama! In fact, I even brought out the black doll he had bought me. I didn't want it when he first gave it to me. I wanted a blonde doll with blue eyes, like all the others had in my class. But he explained, in that quiet gentle way of his, that black was beautiful too and I must learn to be proud of my doll. It didn't make sense to my seven-year-old mind but I had accepted him as 'weird' in any case and so I quietly hid the doll. Three years later, I pulled it out as proof that I was a 'different' daughter of a 'different' father! In fact, I now displayed it with such newfound confidence that instead of being sniggered at by my classmates, I became an object of envy. That was the first lesson he taught me, of turning what is perceived as a disadvantage into a scoring point.

When I opened my eyes to the world, the first colour I saw was red. Till I was nine years old we lived at Red Flag Hall, a commune-like flat of the Communist Party of India (CPI). A huge red flag used to greet visitors at the entrance. It was only later that I realized red was the colour of the worker, of revolution. Each comrade's family had just one room; the bathroom and lavatory was common. Being party members had redefined the husband–wife relationship of the whole group. Most wives were working and it became the responsibility of whichever parent was at home to look after the child. My mother was touring quite a lot with Prithvi Theatre and in her absence Abba would feed, bathe and look after both my brother Baba and me, as a matter of course.

In the beginning, Mummy had to take up a job because all the money Abba earned was handed over to the party. He was allowed to keep only Rs 40 per month which was hardly enough for a family of four. But later when we were monetarily better off and had moved to Janki Kutir, Mummy continued to work in the theatre because she loved being an actor. Once, she was to participate in the Maharashtra State Competition in the title role of *Pagli*. She was completely consumed by the part and would suddenly, without warning, launch into her lines in front of the dhobi, cook, etc. I was convinced she'd gone mad and started weeping with fright. Abba dropped his work and took me for a long walk on the beach. He explained that Mummy had very little time to rehearse her part and that as family it was our duty to make it possible for her to rehearse her lines as many times as she needed to or else she wouldn't win the competition—all this to a nine-year-old child. It made me feel very adult and very included. To this day, whenever my mother is acting in a new play or new film, my father sits up with her and rehearses her cues.

She participates in his life equally; at a price of course! She fell in love with him because he was a poet. However, she learned soon enough that a poet is essentially a man of the people and she would have to share him with his countless admirers (a large number of them female!) and friends. When I was about nine years old, I remember an evening at a big industrialist's home. His wife, a typical socialite, announced in a rather flirtatious manner, 'Kaifi Saheb, my usual *farmaish*, the "*Do Nigahon Ka*" something something . . . You know, folks, Kaifi Saheb has written this nazm in praise of me.' And Abba, without batting an eyelid, started reciting this poem which was in fact written for my mother. I was outraged and started screaming that the poem was written for my mother and not for this stupid woman. A deathly silence prevailed and my mother said, 'Hush, child, hush,' but I am sure *unke dil mein laddoo phoot rahe thay*! Mummy took me into a corner and said that I wasn't to take such things to heart—after all, 'Abba' was a poet and such were his ways—he didn't seriously mean that the poem was written for this lady, etc. I would hear nothing of it. Needless to say, that was a poem Kaifi Azmi could never use again and that woman still hates me!

Amongst his female friends Begum Akhtar was my favourite. She would sometimes stay with us as a houseguest. In fact, Josh Malihabadi, Firaq Gorakhpuri and Faiz Ahmed Faiz would stay with us too despite there being no separate guestroom, not even an attached bathroom. Luxury was never the central concern of these artists; they preferred the warmth of our tiny home to the five-star comforts available to them. I was fascinated by the mehfils at home. I would sit up in rapt attention, not even half understanding what they recited, but excited nevertheless. Their beautiful words fell like music on my young ears. I found the atmosphere fascinating—the steady flow of conversation, the tinkering of glasses, the smoke-filled room. I was never rushed off to bed; in fact I was encouraged to hang around, provided I took the responsibility for getting up in time for school the next day. It made me feel very grown-up and included.

Soon I started attending mushairas—Sahir Ludhianvi was popular, Ali Sardar Jafri greatly respected, but Kaifi Azmi had a different magic. He was always amongst the last to recite, his deeply resonant voice pulsating with vigour, drama and power. Baba and I used to be fast asleep on the stage, behind the *gao-takiyas*, and would invariably wake up to the thunderous applause that resonated each time his name was announced. I never saw him either surprised or flattered by the applause. In fact, to my mother's despair, he would never come home and tell her how the mushaira went. A non-committal '*Theek thha*' was all she could extract from him. Years later, when I was about eighteen, I remember prodding him to tell me which nazm he had recited and what the audience response was like. My mother said briefly, 'Don't even try; he's not going to tell you. Over the years I have trained myself to bury my curiosity in a newspaper when Kaifi comes back from a mushaira.' But I would have none of that. I sat across Abba's chest and tickled him pink till he said, '*Chhichhore log apni tareef karte hain, jis din bura padhoonga, aake bata doonga.*' (Only the lowly sing their own praise; I'll tell you the day I recite badly.)

He never treated his work as special. Even when he came back from a song recording, he never brought the cassette back home. A far cry from young lyricists today, who subject all their guests to their latest song, goading them to say 'Wah-Wah'! He never actually puts pen to paper till the night of the deadline. Then there is a furious cleaning of drawers, numerous letters that get replied to, a number of inconsequential things that get attended to. I'm sure the creative process is occurring simultaneously over the radio blaring, children laughing, children's friends over, *taash* going on in the house. The family is never made to hush up because he is writing; in fact the door of his study is always open so he can keep in touch with the outside world as well. I once changed the position of his desk away from the door because I felt he needed greater privacy. Mummy protested he would hate it. Came evening and predictably Abba made her change it back to the original position. He writes only with a Mont Blanc pen and has a huge collection of them. Every now and again, he takes them all out, looks at them lovingly and then puts them back under lock and key. When a friend of mine presented me one, Abba pinched it although he possessed three identical ones and wrote my friend a 'cute' letter giving reasons why the pen was safer with him than with me!

Few people know that he has a tremendous sense of humour and can be a first-rate mimic. He can laugh repeatedly at family jokes and makes Mummy act out incidents he finds funny again and again. He laughs till tears spill out of his eyes. Looking at his serious face, could anyone believe that!

I was once trying to put his eye drops for him. He has the tiniest little eyes in the world and would blink furiously every time I touched them. Inevitably, the drops would spill over to his nose or ear. Suddenly, he held my hand and started narrating a tale. 'There was a young prince once who was the despair of his father's life because he could do nothing well. The king finally found a marksman who swore he would turn the young prince into a skilled archer. After about six months the prince decided to display his skill. Swish-swosh went his arrows all over the room and felled everything within sight. Finally the king and the teacher decided the only way they could be safe was to stand right in the centre of the target since that was the only place the prince's arrow would never reach!'

When I looked at Abba quizzically to figure out what the story meant, he said with a straight face, '*Apni taraf se tum eye drops mere kaan mein dalo, aankh mein khud-ba-khud pahunch jayenge!*' (Why don't you try putting the eye drops into my ears, I am sure they will reach my eyes on their own.)

He is very fond of good food and cannot eat a meal without gosht. He's hugely 'superior' about being an UP-ite and will not condescend to eat Hyderabadi food, even though Mummy has tried to cajole him over the fifty-two years they've been married! Each time we eat khatti daal, a separate arhar ki daal is cooked for him and woe betide the person who unmindfully picks up the khatti daal ka spoon to serve him his arhar ki daal! He never serves himself and you are never to ask him what he would like to eat. Mummy's trained eye knows almost by a process of osmosis what he should be served and in what quantity. When I protest that this is *dadagiri*, Mummy says she was warned by her mother-in-law that unless she served him, he would get up from the table hungry rather than open his mouth and say *yeh cheez aur chahiye!* The only time he does ask for more is when I cook something. Unfortunately, cooking is not one of my talents and the family runs for miles if they're made to suffer the ordeal of my cooking. But Abba behaves as though he is tasting the best of Avadh's culinary delicacy! He fools nobody but I am touched nevertheless.

There is much that he and Javed have in common. Both have a strong sense of propriety, are extremely *takkaluf-pasand* and cannot brook mediocrity. Both are hugely political animals. I used to deliberately stay away from politics and pride myself on not reading the newspaper as a reaction against all the politics that was discussed constantly in the house. But when I got involved with Javed and heard him and Abba have their discussions (I used to listen from a distance) I gradually started taking an interest. In discovering Javed I was rediscovering Abba, getting in touch once again with Urdu poetry and passionate politics, realizing how deep into my father's ways my roots were.

I got involved with Javed, a married man, which made my mother very unhappy. All my well-wishers predicted disaster for the two of us. All around me there was tremendous pressure to break up with Javed. With my heart pounding I turned to Abba, 'Do you think Javed is the wrong man for me?'

'He is not wrong, his circumstances are,' came the reply.

'But what if he can change the circumstances? Trust me, the marriage was over long before I came into the scene,' I said quietly.

There were no further questions asked. He didn't probe, didn't want to know the details of what that meant. He trusted me enough to take me for my word and gave me his blessings. That was one of the most momentous decisions of my life. Had Abba said no, I wonder if I would have had the courage to defy him—not because I'm frightened of him but because in the most personal of matters he can be relied upon to make the most objective judgement. There are instances without number when I have turned to him for advice. He never gives an opinion unless it is asked for, which is a far cry from Mummy and me who can't help but dole it out mostly to unwilling ears!

In the early years of my career I was so immersed in my films that I knew little about what was happening in the world outside and was content within my own bubble. I remember Tariq Ali and Saeed Akhtar Mirza expressing their dismay at my being such an unworthy daughter but Abba put no pressure on me or ever said, 'You should do this or that.' I think he was confident that *meri mitti itni geeli thhi ke ankur to phootega hi.* (My soil was so fertile that the plant would eventually take root.) And so it did.

My childhood was spent travelling with my mother's Prithvi Theatre on one hand, and on the other, mazdoor kisan meetings in Madanpura with my father. There used to be red banners everywhere, a lot of *naare-baazi* and a lot of protest poetry. As a child I was only interested in these rallies because the labourers pampered me. Imperceptibly, however, my roots were catching soil. The films I was doing started leaving their imprint on me and I started getting involved with women's issues, the rights of the homeless and the need for communal harmony. Today when I'm at a demonstration, participating in a padyatra or in a hunger strike, it is merely an extension of what I saw happening around me as a child.

In 1986, a big slum had been demolished at Cuffe Parade in Bombay to make way for a hostel for MLAs. The slum dwellers had knocked on every door to get alternative accommodation which was their due by law but no one was willing to pay any heed to them. I joined Anand Patwardhan and three slum dwellers from Sanjay Gandhi Nagar on an indefinite hunger strike. On the fourth day of the strike my blood pressure started falling and my mother was beside herself with fear. To her dismay, Abba, who was in Patna, sent me a telegram saying, 'Best of luck, Comrade!'

On another instance I decided to join Swami Agnivesh and Asghar Ali Engineer on a padyatra for communal harmony from Delhi to Meerut. When I went to say goodbye to the family, I was nervous and uncertain. I had been amply warned that it was very dangerous for an actress to be roaming the streets of Uttar Pradesh as my clothes would be ripped off, stones would be thrown, etc. The whole family was reflecting the tension. Mummy, Baba, his wife Tanvi and Javed were all hovering around me but not saying a word. I walked into Abba's room and hugged him from behind. He pulled me up in front of him and said, '*Arrey meri bahadur beti darr rahi hai? Jao, tumhe kuchh nahin hoga.*' His eyes were completely fearless. It was as though a fresh burst of oxygen had been pumped into my bloodstream. Needless to add, the padyatra was a big success. It was yet another instance of my having relied on his judgement and passing the test with flying colours.

As a father, I have always taken Abba for granted, but as a poet I continue to be overwhelmed by his work. I cannot claim to know or even understand all his work but I find his poetry striking for its strong imagery, its sheer power and its broadness of vision. His most personal problem transcends itself in a much larger vision so that his struggle no longer remains his own, but becomes the struggle of all human beings. Whether it's my work with slum dwellers, women or against communalism, there's always a nazm of Abba's to guide me, to inspire me to carry on the struggle. Thus 'Makaan', 'Aurat' and 'Behroopni' have become the pillars on which my work rests.

He is a rare poet who practised what he preached. There is no dichotomy in his life between word and action. The poet who had challenged patriarchy forty-five years ago in his nazm 'Aurat' . . .

> Zindagi jehd mein hai sabr ke qaabu mein nahiin
> Nabz-e-hasti ka lahu kaanpte aansu mein nahiin
> Udne khulne mein hai nikhat kham-e-gesu mein nahiin
> Jannat ik aur hai jo mard ke pahlu mein nahiin
>
> Uss kii azaad ravish par bhii machalna hai tujhe
> Utth meri jaan mere saath hii chalna hai tujhe

. . . had in life, always encouraged his wife, daughter and daughter-in-law to become self-reliant and seek self-fulfilment. The poet who pointed out the irony of the construction worker being turned out of the very building he had built in 'Makaan' . . .

Ban gaya qasr to pehre pe koii baith gaya
So rahe khaaq pe hum shorish-e-tameer liye
Apni nas-nas mein liye mehnat-e-peham kii thakaan
Bund aankhon mein isii qasr kii tasveer liye
Din pighalta hai isii tarah saron par ab tak
Raat aankhon mein khatakti hai siyah teer liye
Aaj kii raat bahut garm havaa chaltii hai
Aaj kii raat naa footpath pe neend aaegii
Sab utho, main bhi uthuun, tum bhii utho, tum bhii utho
Koii khirkii isii diivaar mein khul jaaegii

. . . has continued to live in a rented house in Bombay. The poet who wrote '*Behroopni*', a frightening poem on communalism, was out there marching on the streets in Ayodhya, during the height of the Babri Masjid—Ram Janmabhoomi dispute, while others were content to condemn the upsurge of communalism at cocktail parties or five-star seminars.

This is the story of a man who has lived his life fully and at eighty-two is raring to go. When he had his paralytic stroke on that fateful day of 8 February 1973, we thought his work would have to take a back seat. Five days after coming out of coma, barely able to speak, he dictated the poem '*Dhamak*' to Shama Zaidi, describing the explosion of his brain haemorrhage. A month later he had written, whilst still in hospital, the poem '*Zindagi*'. It starts with a man lying on his deathbed.

Aaj andhera meri nas-nas mein utar jayega
Aankhen bujh jayengi bujh jayenge ehsas-o-shaoor
Aur ye sadiyon se jalta sa sulagta sa wajood
Isse pehle ki sahar mathe pe shabnam chhidke
Isse pehle ke meri beti ke woh phool se haath
Garm rukhsar ko thandak baqshein

Isse pehle ke mere bete ka mazboot badan
Tann-e-maflooj mein shakti bhar de
Isse pehle ki meri biwi ke honth
Mere honthon ki tapish pi jayein
Raakh ho jayega jalte
Aur phir raakh raakh bikhar jaayegi

The poem, however, does not end on a note of despair. It traces man's struggle over the years to conquer death and analyses how religion became a means to conquer man's fear of the unknown.

Maut lehrati thi sau shaklon mein
Maine ghabrake har shakl ko Khuda maan liya

Finally he comes back to the man on the hospital bed, revitalized and invigorated, ready to face life anew.

You find again and again in Kaifi's poetry the ability to rise above the personal and encompass a much larger vision, so that his struggle is not his alone but becomes the struggle of all humanity. It is impossible to arrive at any understanding of Kaifi Azmi, unless you include his work for Mijwan, the tiny village in Azamgarh where he was born and has now decided to spend the rest of his life.

Abba, who had left Mijwan in his teens, returned briefly to it when he married Mummy and had his first child Khayyam (a son who died at the age of one). Soon after Partition, his family migrated to Pakistan one by one and he felt his roots in Mijwan had been severed forever. However, in 1973, upon partially recovering from his brain haemorrhage, his left side still severely damaged, he started chanting the name 'Mijwan' with such persistence that my mother was forced to take him there. It turned out to be an amazing trip for him. He realized that Mijwan was and would always remain the place where he belonged. The house he was born in was occupied by various distant cousins and it would have been unfair to throw them out (the communist theory of the tiller owning the land). Kaifi wrote in anguish.

> *Woh mera gaon hai*
> *Woh mere gaon ke chulhe*
> *Ke jin mein sholay to sholay*
> *Dhuan nahin milta*

Today, Mijwan is a model village, but it has been a long and arduous journey filled with obstacles that he had to face from vested interests. It fills me with immense pride that once he committed himself to something he never wavered no matter what adversity came his way. I have grown up believing that merely good intentions are not enough, you have to translate them into action.

I once asked him, 'Abba, don't you get frustrated when change doesn't happen at the pace you want it to?'

He answered with equanimity, '*Bete*, when you are working for change, you should build into that expectation the possibility that the change might not happen in your lifetime. But you must have the conviction that if you carry on working with dedication, the change is bound to occur, even if it does so after you are gone.'

His prophetic words have become my mantra in the work that I do with the weak and the dispossessed.

Postscript: 10 June 2002

I look out of the window from Abba's room. The sky is blue, the grass green, flowers in bloom. I turn back to look inside the room. Books lined neatly on the shelves, his spectacles, writing pad, Mont Blanc lie in wait for pen to be put to paper and new verse to flow . . . everything is the way it was . . . but Abba is not there . . .

Anees Jung, in a letter of condolence to me, writes, 'I know what the loss of a parent means, Shabana. I also know one never loses a parent. In a strange mystical way they become closer in death, for their spirit, no longer trapped in a frail frame, becomes all pervasive and surrounds us like the air we breathe.'

Comforting words no doubt but all I feel is insurmountable grief.

Abba was not only my father, he was my friend, my mentor, my guru. In the last few months of his illness, as he lay in the ICU with tubes down his stomach, throat and neck, he could not speak and yet we managed to communicate. He would raise his eyebrow, squeeze my hand, indicate with his eyes and I would understand. In the same way that I understand what our granddaughter Shakya wants, although she is not yet able to speak. Abba, in any case, was given to long silences. He spoke both through his words and through his silences.

He fell silent much before the tubes were physically put into him. The Gujarat carnage shattered him. I would watch him as he looked at the television coverage, face frozen in pain. Tears streaming down my eyes, I asked, 'Don't you feel frustrated and defeated as you see the mindless killing, the hateful revenge, man killing man in the name of religion?' He wiped my tears and said quietly, 'The riots are not spontaneous, they have been engineered for narrow political gain. The common man craves *roti, kapda aur makaan* irrespective of the faith he follows. This madness will pass.'

It was his faith, his belief in the innate goodness of man that kept him going through the darkest of times. I am trying hard to keep my faith in his faith.

Pyaar ka jashn nai tarah manaanaa hogaa
Gham kisi dil mein sahi gham ko mitaanaa hogaa

In the effort of wiping the tears of the victims of the Gujarat carnage and thousands of others who have fallen prey to communal riots, in wiping the tears of slum dwellers constantly displaced by mindless government policies, in wiping the tears of all marginalized sections of society, particularly women, can I pay tribute to my father, a giant amongst men?

Koi to sood chukaye koi to zimma ley
Uss inquilab ka jo aaj tak udhaar sa hai

You envelope me like the air I breathe, Abba. I promise to turn my personal loss into an armour like you had always done, and carry on with the work you left behind. You are watching over us, aren't you?

A decade and a half later . . .

Fifteen years later I am returning from Mijwan with Namrata by my side and a whole host of her young friends from Mumbai who have been actively involved with the Mijwan Welfare Society for the last ten years.

The tiny village that didn't even exist on the map of India is now a global name ever since the leading Bollywood couturier Manish Malhotra started getting chikankari (a delicate hand embroidery that is the pride of Awadh) crafted by the women of Mijwan. All leading Hindi film stars from Shah Rukh Khan to Deepika Padukone have been show-stoppers at the annual Mijwan fashion shows. Ranbir Kapoor is our goodwill ambassador. Mijwan is now a brand that shines in golden letters.

But more importantly there has been a sea change in the attitude of the villagers. The shackles of a deeply patriarchal society are being broken . . .

Tod yeh azm-shikan daghdagha-e-pand bhi tod

. . . and women are negotiating greater space for themselves. With financial independence coming their way, the status quo within families has changed. Women have their own bank accounts and are equal participants in the decision-making process both within the family and within the community. The scourge of child marriage which was rampant in Mijwan and its surrounding villages is now a thing of the past. This was the mindset change Kaifi had worked towards.

A bright student from Kaifi Azmi Girls Inter College, Mijwan, Shweta Prajapati, thought nothing of washing dishes at a relative's house because hers was the last mud hut in the village and she wanted to gift her parents a pukka house. She is now studying at the Mahatma Gandhi International University in Wardha. She says confidently, 'There is nothing that a girl cannot do. All she needs is opportunity. Thank you, Mijwan, for giving me that opportunity.'

Lalima used to trudge 8 kilometres every day from her village to the school in Mijwan, so determined was she to educate herself. Today she cycles to the embroidery centre and earns enough to look after her ailing parents and educate her younger sister. Her eyes shining, she says, 'Mijwan has taught me to dream big. I am determined to achieve success and bring glory to my country.'

In two months from now, Baba will be making his first feature film *Mee Raqsam*, with Aditi from Mijwan playing the fourteen-year-old protagonist. She is the younger daughter of Gopal who was Abba's loyal attendant till the very end. How empowering for Aditi and how aspirational for the young women of Mijwan who have opened beauty parlours, walked the ramp along with Shah Rukh Khan and Ranbir Kapoor and can now look forward to acting as a career.

All along, Baba had resisted the lure of Mijwan. He was unhappy that Abba had given up the comforts of Mumbai to settle in a tiny village that didn't have any health facilities. As was his wont Abba never argued with Baba because deep down he was confident that the prodigal son would return. As he did inevitably and inexorably. By using Mijwan as the background for his first film, Baba pays the biggest tribute he could have to his father.

All this would have pleased Kaifi no doubt but he was not one for resting on laurels . . . I can see him up and about, heading towards the next goal . . .

India is changing, Abba, some for good, some for bad. There is an attempt to curb freedom of expression, to frighten people into silence, to not express dissent. You had faced various such challenges and you stood up to them boldly. Today it seems as though many artists are buckling under, buying tremulous peace. But when it seems dark and bleak I recall your words, 'Do not succumb to despair, to this night a dawn there just has to be.' When I see young men and women putting themselves out there to offer resistance, unbridled, unafraid, I recall your lines from 'Charaaghan':

. . . haan magar ek diya naam hai jiska ummeed
Jhilmilata hi chala jaata hai . . .

. . . yes, but there's a light called hope
That keeps burning bright

Shabana Azmi
December 2018

Introduction

A child was born to a family of zamindars in the village of Mijwan in district Azamgarh (Uttar Pradesh) on 14 January 1919. He was named Saiyyed Athar Husain; in later years he would call himself Kaifi Azmi and carry a bit of his beloved Azamgarh with him all his life. Shortly after the child's birth, his father Saiyyed Fateh Hussain Rizvi decided to leave the lands and fields in Mijwan in the care of his younger brother and move to Lucknow in search of a better life and education for his children. The ties with the village, however, would never snap; the father built a large house in the village from the money he earned in the city and the son spent the last fifteen years of his life in Mijwan, transforming the sleepy little hamlet into a model village, a task continued to this day by the third generation, thus keeping intact the link with the land and its people in an almost unbroken arc spanning close to a century.

A young Kaifi had watched his four older sisters die of tuberculosis as his parents tried to get the best possible medical attention for them to no avail. This early exposure to disease and death made him inward, reflective, even 'gham-pasand' ('liking sorrow') in his own words. Fearful that none of his surviving children would be familiar with their religion or culture, Kaifi's father decided that Kaifi should be given religious instruction in a madrasa unlike his elder brothers who had been sent to the Aligarh University. And so Kaifi began his formal education at the Sultan-ul Madaris, the largest Shia seminary in Lucknow, as a boarder. It was here that he first heard of the incendiary collection *Angarey* ('Sparks') and had his first encounter with progressivism.[1] It was here, too, that the seeds of his later activism were laid; first, when he set up a students' body to address the needs of fellow students and present them to the administration, and then when he launched a year-long strike to ensure that their demands were met. Already fond of writing poetry, having composed his first ghazal at the age of eleven,[2]

---

[1] In the introduction to his collected works, *Kaifiyaat*, Kaifi describes this encounter; as a young boy freshly arrived from the village, he pushes a stool against a small high window and peers into a small room in the Shia seminary. He sees his maulvi sahab lying in bed and two or three other maulvis sitting huddled around him while a young boy, the same age as Kaifi, is reading aloud from *Angarey*. All through the reading, the maulvi saheb would exclaim '*Lahaoul willa quwwat...*' to express his horror and disapproval of the book's contents and pinch the hapless boy's cheeks simultaneously. *Angarey*, comprising nine short stories and one play by four young writers namely, Sajjad Zaheer, Ahmad Ali, Mahmud-uz-Zafar and Dr Rashid Jahan, was published in December 1932 and banned by the colonial administration in March 1933 in the face of fierce condemnation from Muslims, especially the Shia community, for hurting their religious sentiments. The government of the United Provinces confiscated and burnt as many copies of the book as it could; the handful that survived were read surreptitiously. The secrecy about the book, and the desire to read it despite the directives (both religious and lay) not to, added to the intrigue and drama behind *Angarey*.

[2] This ghazal, '*Itna to zindagi mein kisi ki khalal padey/Hansne se ho sukun na roney se kal padey*', was composed by Kaifi and recited at a mushaira

the strike compelled Kaifi to write *inquilabi* (revolutionary) and *ehtejaji* (protest) poetry.[3] And thus was forged a poetic temperament that brought together, almost instinctively, the radical and the progressive with the lyrical and the romantic.

While agitating for the rights of his fellow students at the Sultan-ul Madaris, Kaifi met a galaxy of intellectuals in Lucknow: first and foremost the leading Urdu writer, Ali Abbas Hussaini, who in turn, introduced him to Ehtesham Husain, the foremost Marxist critic and academic; Azam Husain, the editor of the daily *Sarfaraz*; and Ali Sardar Jafri, the firebrand student leader and budding poet who would remain a lifelong friend and comrade. By now, having abandoned all plans of becoming a maulvi, Kaifi continued his studies in Arabic and Persian by taking several private examinations. As poetry and politics began to play an increasing role in his life, his goal of sitting for the F.A. examination as a private candidate and eventually studying in a college was thwarted. Kaifi got drawn into the nationwide agitation for swaraj (self-rule) and satyagraha (the civil disobedience movement) launched by Mahatma Gandhi. He began to join the *prabhat pheri* processions, reciting his own poetry as he went from house to house at the break of dawn.[4]

---

at Bahraich. It was received very enthusiastically by the audience and eventually reached Begum Akhtar who set it to music and turned it into a nationwide phenomenon in pre-partition India.

[3] Kaifi talks of writing at least one poem every day during the strike to foster a sense of solidarity and fervour among his fellow students. These years at the madrasa would prove to be defining ones in an entirely unexpected way, one that his parents could never have foreseen when they sent him to train to be a maulvi.

[4] He wrote several nazms such as '*Utho dekho woh aandhi aa rahi hai*' that were later published in *Jhankaar* during these years and recited them during the *prabhat pheri*. Gandhi-ji adopted the *prabhat pheri*, literally

His first brush with the police came when he was building a bonfire of imported clothes in front of a textile shop in Lucknow's Aminabad neighbourhood. Later, when he moved to Kanpur and came in contact with the labour unions, his contact with the communist party strengthened and his world view became more sharply polarized between the privileged and the unprivileged. Soon his poems began to be published—both in literary magazines and in overtly left-leaning journals such as *Qaumi Jung*, edited by Sajjad Zaheer in faraway Bombay, a city that was fast establishing itself as the beating heart of the new and vibrant Progressive Writers' Movement (PWM).

While still a lad cutting his teeth as a poet, Kaifi had decided that if he were to make a name for himself outside the hinterland, in the glittering mushaira circuit of the big cities, he could not remain un-mentored and untutored; like all good poets, he would need *islah* (correction) from an ustad (teacher). And so he sought out Maulana Safi, one of the leading ustad poets in Lucknow. Safi saheb heard the young poet recite '*Itna to zindagi mein kisi ki khalal padey/Hansne se ho sukun na roney se kal padey*' and, instead of taking him on as a disciple, offered words of sage counsel that would remain with Kaifi all his life. Maulana Safi cautioned him against the pitfalls of the wah-wahs and the adulation that can lead one astray; instead, he urged the boy to keep reading and writing. The flaws in his writing would shed themselves like dry leaves, the master said, and the

---

meaning 'morning stroll', but comprising songs and slogans recited by volunteers at the crack of dawn to awaken people and also as a tool for spreading information about self-rule, civil disobedience, etc., through songs and slogans in order to be accessible and easily understood by ordinary people. Gandhi-ji's use of the *prabhat pheri* was an unorthodox but highly effective tool of propaganda.

strengths would keep sprouting like fresh new leaves. And so it happened . . .

In the course of a poetic career spanning over six decades, awards and encomiums followed Kaifi in ample measure: there was the Padma Shri, India's fourth-highest civilian award; the Uttar Pradesh Urdu Academy Award and the Sahitya Akademi Award for Urdu for his collection *Awaara Sajdey* in 1975, Special Award of Maharashtra Urdu Academy, Soviet Land Nehru Award, Lotus Award from the Afro-Asian Writers' Association, and President's Award for National Integration. In 1998, the Government of Maharashtra conferred the Jyaneshwara Award on him. He was also honoured with the prestigious Sahitya Akademi Fellowship for lifetime achievement in 2002. In 2000, he was conferred the first Millennium Award by the Government of Delhi and the Delhi Urdu Academy and a doctorate from the Visva Bharati University in Santiniketan. He won the National Film Award in 1970 for Best Lyrics for the film *Saat Hindustani* and the National Award and Filmfare Award in 1975 for the screenplay (with Shama Zaidi) and dialogue (with Ismat Chughtai) for M.S. Sathyu's iconic Partition saga, *Garam Hawa*.

* * *

Kaifi wrote roughly 240 songs for eighty films. His career as a *naghma-nigaar* (lyricist) began with the song 'Rotey rotey guzar gayi raat re' for the film *Buzdil* (1951), produced by Shahid Latif, the husband of fellow Urdu writer Ismat Chughtai. The last songs he possibly wrote were for the film *Chand Grahan* (1997). His non-film poetic oeuvre comprises four collections: *Jhankaar* (1944), *Akhir-e Shab* (1947), *Awaara Sajdey* (1973) and *Iblis ki Majlis-e Shuura: Doosra Ijlaas* (1983). All his non-film poetry can be found in his collected works *Kaifiyaat*, and all his film lyrics are to be found in Devanagari in *Meri Awaaz Suno*. Taken together, they showcase a poetic vocabulary that drew from the classical idiom of Urdu poetry yet kept inventing new and modern ways of expressing timeless emotions.

Javed Akhtar is related to Kaifi by bonds other than marriage too. He is, of course, Kaifi's son-in-law but is also the son of fellow progressive poet, Jan Nisar Akhtar and Safiya Akhtar, also a fine writer. From his mother's side, he is the nephew of Urdu's most romantically revolutionary poet, Majaz. Like Kaifi, Javed Akhtar shares the catholic, all-encompassing world view that was once so typical of the *qasbati* culture of Uttar Pradesh. Pointing out the inextricable link between Kaifi's poetry and the person he was, Akhtar says, 'He was a strange man. Unlike other lofty poets, his writing, his poetry, his life and his thinking were all resonant of each other. This is not easy to do.' In fact, Javed Akhtar's tribute to Kaifi, titled appropriately enough 'Ajeeb Aadmi Tha Woh' ('He was a Strange Man'), lists the many combinations of contraries that came together in a very harmonious way. Indeed, Kaifi's life and work mirror each other in a remarkable way and to a remarkable degree.

Given that Kaifi once said that writing film lyrics is a task akin to first digging a grave and then looking for a corpse to fit in, he managed to do a more than competent job of not merely writing on a given *dhun* (melody) but also bringing in his own world view. Plagued as the film industry is with rampant populism and constrained as the very craft of writing lyrics for cinema is by context and commercial considerations, Kaifi managed to find work with like-minded people. His association with Chetan Anand was especially fruitful in a spate of spectacular films for which he wrote some hauntingly lyrical songs: *Hanste Zakhm, Hindustan ki Kasam, Heer Ranjha, Aakhri Khat* and *Haqeeqat.*

Coming to his non-film poetry, several of Kaifi's nazms are written for the people in his life who were important to him or for others from the public domain whom he held in high esteem. For instance, there's 'Shaguftgi ki latafat ka shahkaar ho tum' for his wife, Shaukat, as well as the short poem, 'Shaukat ke Naam', that he uses as a dedication to Awaara Sajdey. Then, there's 'Ab aur kya dega tera bimar baap tujhko' that's clearly written for his daughter Shabana or 'Waseeat' ('Will') for his son, Baba. Some have apocryphal stories attached to them such as the nazm entitled 'Pashemani' ('Main yeh soch kar uss ke dar se uttha tha') said to be inspired by an early love written on leaving Lucknow for Kanpur which he then gave to Chetan Anand to be used in the film Haqeeqat with minor tweaking.[5] There are poems inspired by Sarojini Naidu, Jawaharlal Nehru, Stalin, Lenin and a jewel-like ode for Christ entitled 'Ibn-e Maryam'.

A visit to the motherland of organized communism, the USSR, inspires a slew of poems such as 'Moscow', 'Ferghana', 'Tashkent' written in the summer of 1969. There are others written on Korea and Beirut. Sir Muhammad Iqbal's famous poem 'Iblis ki Majlis-e Shuura' ('The Parliament of Satan') written in 1935 constituted a scathing indictment of the socio-economic paradigm offered by the West; Kaifi's long poem with the same name, written approximately fifty years later, takes the story of inequities forward, bringing in topical concerns such as the growing hegemonic power of the United States, the threat of nuclear warfare, rampant consumerism, heedless capitalism, etc. Like a master vintner pouring new wine in old bottles, Kaifi has used traditional genres such as the qataa, masnavi and the ghazal to speak of radically new concerns; there is, for instance, the

---

[5] Sumantra Ghosal recording

long ballad-like *masnavi* '*Khana Jungi*' ('Civil War') and '*Awaam*' ('People').

While Kaifi wrote several ghazals, it is in the nazm that he felt able to say more and to say it in his own inimitable style. Being a new genre, one that the progressive poets can rightfully claim to have made their own, the nazm is capacious enough to make overtly political statements. Several of Kaifi's poems are inspired by contemporary events such as the creation of Bangladesh, the disturbances in Telangana, a province in the erstwhile princely state of Hyderabad that was of special interest to the communist party because of its large peasant population and agrarian unrest. The breaking of the domes of the mosque in Ayodhya in December 1992 caused Kaifi to write the poignant '*Doosra Banwas*' referring to Ram leaving Ayodhya a second time. Then there's '*Makaan*' ('House'), one of his most quoted nazms with its rousing determination to arise and take collective action against oppression:

Aaj kii raat bahut garm havaa chaltii hai
Aaj kii raat naa footpath pe neend aaegii
Sab utho, main bhi uthuun, tum bhii utho, tum bhii utho
Koii khirkii isii diivaar mein khul jaaegii

Tonight a blistering wind blows
It will not let us sleep on the footpath
Come, let us get up, you, me, all of us
A window will open in this wall

Shabana talks of her father not merely with love and admiration, as a daughter would, but also with great vim and vigour.[6]

---

[6] Shabana Azmi, Interview

Kaifi comes alive in her telling of incidents relating to her father's life or poetic career. Conversations with her tend to throw light not merely on incidents from her father's life or why and when a particular poem or film lyric was written but also on the nuts and bolts of poetry itself. For instance, she describes how two film lyricists will describe a given situation in two vastly different ways given their own world view. For the film *Ek Pal*, Kaifi writes '*Aane wali hai bahaar*' on the birth of a child to an unwed mother. For the same situation, Gulzar writes, '*Jaane kya hai ji darta hai, ro deney ko ji karta hai*'. She also talks of the unfailing optimism that limned Kaifi's view of the world, an intrinsic belief in a better future. This can possibly be attributed to Kaifi's inherently socialist world view.

How did the son of a zamindar, born in a feudal family in rural Azamgarh, educated in a madrasa in Lucknow, acquire this sharply political world view? For this, we must briefly digress to take in the importance of a powerful literary grouping that left an enduring mark on the intellectual landscape of India.

* * *

The significance of the PWM and the Progressive Writers' Association (PWA), known in Urdu as *Anjuman-i Taraqqui Pasand Mussannifin*, is uncontested for most commentators on the literary history of India. It succeeded in bringing into its fold established and emerging writers from almost all the important languages in the Indian subcontinent. Virtually from its inception, it succeeded in gaining the attention—and the blessings—of the literary stalwarts of the time. Rabindranath Tagore, Dr Muhammad Iqbal, Maulvi Abdul Haq, Hasrat Mohani, Acharya Narendra Dev, Tara Chand and Sarojini Naidu, while belonging to diverse literary traditions, endorsed the PWM and its objectives. The eminent Hindi writer Premchand addressed the inaugural session of the First All-India Progressive Writers' Association in Lucknow on 9 April 1936, virtually spelling out its agenda in his presidential speech entitled '*Sahitya ka Uddeshya*' ('The Purpose of Literature').

In the years ahead, some of the greatest Urdu writers came to be associated with it, namely Faiz Ahmed Faiz, Sajjad Zaheer, Ismat Chughtai, Krishan Chandar, Kaifi Azmi, Ali Sardar Jafri among others. The importance of this movement today lies not merely in the intrinsic merits of the writers associated with it or their individual works; it lies instead in the role played by the PWA—and its partner organization, the Indian People's Theatre Association (IPTA)—from the mid-1930s till the mid-1950s in shaping the political consciousness of large numbers of people, in its unequivocal emphasis on the need for social change and in the relentless portrayal of these twin forces in their literature, and by extension in all forms of art and popular culture.

The movement and its proponents soon became a powerful and inescapable force commandeering a space for themselves on the political, social and literary canvas of India for nearly three decades. In the years before Independence, they influenced the debates on imperialism and decolonization and in the years after they were at the centre of the discourses on the nature of the newly independent, post-colonized state and society. While the PWA was a pan-Indian movement with flourishing branches in all the major Indian cities, Bombay was the beating heart of the PWM, and it was here that the movement flourished and reached its zenith. What the writers in the Bombay branch of the PWA thought or wrote or included in the journals they edited or the many anthologies they published impacted writers across the length and breadth of India. How did this come to be?

By 1944, a large number of progressive writers had begun to flock to Bombay. Josh Malihabadi, Akhtar ul Iman, Krishan Chandar and Saghar Nizami were in Poona, but the lure of the silver screen drew them to the city that was home to the biggest film industry in Asia. By the time the Second World War ended, some of the most dynamic writers of the age had gathered in Bombay from different parts of undivided India: among the Urdu writers there were Rajinder Singh Bedi, Hameed Akhtar, Sardar Jafri, Kaifi Azmi, Jan Nisar Akhtar, Majrooh Sultanpuri, Rifat Sarosh, Niyaz Haider, Hajra Masrur and Khadija Mastur, Saadat Hasan Manto, Miraji, Vishwamitra Adil, Ismat Chughtai and her husband Shahid Latif to name a few; Hindi writers Upendranath Askh, Nemichandra Jain, Amritlal Nagar, Balraj Sahni, Prem Dhawan; Marathi writers Mama Warerkar and Anna Bhau Sathe; and Gujarati writers Bakulesh Swapnath and Bhogilal Gandhi.

It is to this Bombay that Kaifi Azmi brought his Hyderabadi bride, Shaukat Azmi, to live in the commune in Andheri. Kaifi had met Shaukat in Hyderabad where he had gone to attend a mushaira and promptly fallen in love. Shaukat records her meeting with Kaifi, her marriage to him despite the differences in the family background and status, her arrival in Bombay to live as the wife of a comrade in a commune in her memoir *Yaad ki Rehguzar* ('The Pathway of Memory'). Shaukat notes her first impressions thus: 'We went to Kaifi's tiny room . . . there was a loosely strung jute *charpai* with a *dhurrie*, a mattress, a sheet, a pillow . . . a chair . . . some books, piles of newspapers, a mug and a glass. The simplicity of this room touched my heart . . .'[7]

---

[7] *Kaifi & I: A Memoir*, Translated from the Urdu by Nasreen Rahman, New Delhi: Zubaan, 2010, p. 44.

Shaukat provides a luminous account of her new life in the company of gregarious comrades: Zaheer and his wife Razia and their two daughters, the affable duo of Muneesh and Mehdi,[8] Jafri and his wife Sultana who took Shaukat under her wing and taught her the ways of coping in a commune; the parsimonious Party Treasurer Comrade Ghate (who nevertheless grudgingly parted with Rs 100 to the newly-weds); and P.C. Joshi who comes across in her narrative as a benevolent despot. Shaukat's nikah with Kaifi was witnessed by nearly all the progressive writers from Bombay; it was followed, naturally enough, by a mushaira with Majaz reciting 'Aaj ki Raat' ('Tonight') and the bride being presented a copy of the groom's second collection of poetry, 'Aakhir-e-Shab' ('The End of the Night'), dedicated

---

[8] In a lengthy interview with S.M. Mehdi, who had retired to live in Aligarh till he passed away in 2015, I was able to get corroboration of Shaukat's account. Like Shaukat, he blamed B.T. Ranadive, who took over from Joshi in 1947, for the infighting and bitterness that marred the post-1947 years. Mehdi also told me how Muneesh, Kaifi and he formed a trio in the commune. In the course of a rambling chat, he described the party leadership as being puritan, bent upon keeping the party away from *badnami* (getting a bad name). He also described how the party tolerated neither bohemianism nor 'deviations' such as homosexuality. One of Mehdi's designated tasks was to distribute the Urdu weekly *Naya Zamana* in the Muslim areas of Mohammed Ali Road and Bhindi Bazar. Bitterly critical of Ranadive, he claimed, the sectarianism fostered by him eventually led to the split in the party. In contrast, he praised P.C. Joshi for his inclusive policies. He described Joshi as critical of the national leadership but not anti-nationalistic, the way Mehdi perceived Ranadive's policies to be. Joshi, he believed, did not want to cut off the communist movement from the nationalist movement and kept his links open with Gandhi and Nehru. Ranadive, on the other hand, was vehemently opposed to this, deeming the independence that was finally achieved a 'false freedom'.

to her. Shaukat describes Kaifi and his friends, who would become her fellow-travellers, thus: 'They were enlightened and humane individuals who were struggling to create a new world for the poor, the destitute and the hungry. Although they were from different parts of India, these people were like one family where everyone was addressed as "Comrade", which at the time meant an evolved human being.'[9]

Kaifi earned Rs 40 as monthly salary from the party; from this he had to give Rs 30 towards his wife's boarding expense. To earn some extra money, he wrote a column for the Urdu daily, *Jamhuriat* (Democracy).[10] Partly to lighten the burden on Kaifi and partly in response to P.C. Joshi's command that 'the wife of a communist should never sit idle', Shaukat got drawn into the IPTA.[11] Her first role was in Ismat Chughtai's *Dhani Bankein* ('Green Bangles'), a play on the Hindu–Muslim riots that were

---

[9] *Kaifi & I*, op. cit., p. 49.

[10] From 1956 onwards, Kaifi had a fairly successful stint as a film lyricist with films like *Yahudi ki Beti, Kagaz ke Phool, Anupama, Haqeeqat, Pakeezah, Heer Ranjha, Hanste Zakhm, Garam Hawa, Razia Sultan*, etc. Several Urdu writers came to Bombay all through the 1940s to find work in the film industry—as scriptwriters, lyricists, film journalists—and met with varying degrees of success. Kaifi had a better stint than most of them in the film industry.

[11] IPTA was launched on May 1943 in Bombay with Joshi as president and Anil de Silva as general secretary with the aim of using the stage and other traditional arts to portray the problems facing the country. Joshi had earlier begun the practice of gathering the country's prominent writers, journalists, artists, economists, historians, film and stage actors to rally around the party organ, *National Front*, and later *People's War* and *People's Age*. He commissioned Sunil Jana to take photographs of the Bengal famine and document people's movements in different parts of the country, such as in Telangana. Joshi understood, and capitalized on, the need to use culture as a living tool. While the catalyst for IPTA

tearing the fabric of a newly independent India. Here, Shaukat got involved in the country's most vigorous cultural movement that had the likes of Zohra Segal, Uzra Butt, Bhisham Sahni, Prithviraj Kapoor among its stalwarts.

The IPTA, the PWA and the Bombay film industry were like three interlinked circles, with overlapping memberships and a host of common concerns. Foremost among these was a socially transformative agenda which would fulfil the needs of a fledgling nation. For this they sought inspiration not only from Marxist tomes and ideologues but also from Nehruvian socialism that hailed schools, colleges, dams and factories as the 'temples of modern India'. Members of IPTA and PWA— some of whom worked in the film industry as actors, directors, scriptwriters, lyricists, technicians, etc.—worked in tandem to produce a radically new set of images, metaphors, vocabulary, even aesthetics that influenced several generations of filmgoers. Their most visible and immediate effect was the introduction of a non-sectarian ethos, one that rose above the narrow confines of caste, creed and religion and worked as balm on a national psyche that had been traumatized by the communal outrages before, after and during the partition.

The hegemonic ideological force of the PWA in Bombay did not dissipate overnight. The coming of Independence saw the departure of many writers to Pakistan, especially Zaheer who was sent by the Communist Party of India (CPI) to set up the communist party in Pakistan. The declaration of Independence as false freedom by the CPI and the increasing ideological commitment demanded by Jafri alienated many. The flock dwindled, many of the progressive journals closed

---

was the Bengal famine, it continued to be active long after the PWA declined.

down, Urdu itself shrunk in importance as a lingua franca. Those who remained within the progressives' fold increasingly found no reason *not* to respond to Nehru's call and join the nation-building project. Then, in purely literary terms, there was the rise of another literary movement—the modernist movement—that spoke of the inner life, the life of the mind. The PWA, as it had existed in all its glory and might all through the 1940s, became a shadow of its former self. Having said that, while the Bombay progressives may have weakened as a literary group, their influence continued to be felt for a very long time in the work of the film lyricists. For instance, Kaifi was speaking for an entire generation of progressives when he was writing for films such as *Apna Haath Jagannath* (1960):

Apne haath ko pehchaan . . .
Haath uthhatey hain jo kudaal, parbat kaat giratey hain
Jungal se khetii ki taraf morh ke dariya latey hain

Know the power of your hand . . .
The hand that lifts the pickaxe, can cut down mountains
And turn the river away from the forests into your fields

In K.A. Abbas's *Saat Hindustani* (1969)[12] we see Kaifi exhorting his fellow countrymen and women—almost in Soviet style—to move forward and build a new and prosperous India:

---

[12] This film is significant for several reasons: Directed by K.A. Abbas and based on a story by Abbas himself, it starred Amitabh Bachchan who made his debut in the Hindi film industry with this film. *Saat Hindustani* won the Nargis Dutt Award for Best Feature Film on National Integration and fetched Kaifi his first National Film Award for Best Lyrics.

Zulm hadd se badheyga to ghatt jayega
Apni talwaar se aap kat jayega . . .
Yuun badho jaisey lehra ke dhaara badhey
Thokrein khaaye to dil hamara badhey

Tyranny will diminish when it exceeds its limits
It will be cut by its own sword . . .
Move forward like the boisterous wave
Heartbreaks only make my heart stronger

And in the same film:

Faasle sab dilon ke mitaatey chalo
Apne seene se sabko lagatey chalo

Move forward, removing distances between hearts
Meet others, embrace them as you move forward

In *Naunihal* (1967), Kaifi celebrates the enduring legacy of
Nehru whom he has long admired with this ode to Nehru's
liberal humanism which he believes is the balm that a country
scarred from post-partition desperately needs:

Meri awaaz suno, pyaar ka saaz suno . . .

Kyun sajaii hai yeh chandan ki chita mere liye
Main koi jism nahiin hoon ke jala dogey mujhey
Raakh ke saath bikhar jaaoonga main duniya mein
Tum jahaan khaaoge thokar wahiin paogey mujhey

Hear my voice, listen to the song of love . . .

Why have you set up this sandalwood pyre for me
I am not just a body that you can burn me to ashes
I will scatter in the world with my ashes
When you stumble you will find me beside you

* * *

Writing the foreword to the first collection of Kaifi's poems, Sajjad Zaheer, the influential progressive ideologue, writer and general secretary of the PWA wrote: 'A new flower has bloomed in the garden of modern Urdu poetry, a red flower.' Critique of fascism, imperialism, capitalism blend and merge seamlessly with vignettes of love, longing and loss. The first collection contains some of his most enduringly popular nazms such as 'Aurat' and 'Taj Mahal'; the latter which does not feature in the pages of this volume deserves to be quoted in full here not least for its lyricism as also for its unconventional response to the spectacular beauty of an emperor's monument of love by a very young man. It carries a portent of Kaifi's lifelong belief in socialism:

Dost! Main dekh chuka Taj Mahal
   . . . vapas chal

Marmarin marmarin phulon se ubalta hira
   Chand ki aanch mein dahke hue simin minar
   Zehn-e-shair se ye karta hua chashmak paiham
   Ik malika ka ziya-posh o faza-tab mazar

Khud ba-khud phir gae nazron mein ba-andaz-e-saval
   Woh jo raaston pe padey rahte hain lashon ki tarah

Khushk ho kar jo simat jaate hain be-ras aasab
Dhuup mein khopdiyan bajti hain tashon ki tarah

Dost! Main dekh chuka Taj Mahal
. . . vapas chal

Yeh dhadakta hua gumbad mein dil-e-Shahjahan
Yeh dar-o-baam pe hansta hua malika ka shabab
Jagmagata hai har ik tah se mazaq-e-tafriq
Aur tarikh uddhati hai mohabbat ki naqab

Chandni aur ye mahal alam-e-hairat ki qasam
Dudh ki nahr mein jis tarah ubaalaa jaaye
Aise sayyah ki nazron mein khupe kya ye saman
Jisko Farhaad ki qismat ka khayal aa jaaye

Dost! Main dekh chuka Taj Mahal
. . . vapas chal

Ye damakti hui chaukhat ye tila-posh kalas
Inhin jalvon ne diya qabr-parasti ko rivaj
Maah-o anjum bhi hue jaate hain majbur-e-sujud
Vaah araam-gah-e-malika-e-maabud-mizaj

Didani qasr nahin didani taqsim hai ye
Ru-e-hasti pe dhuan qabr pe raqs-e-anvar
Phail jaaye isi rauza ka jo simta daaman
Kitne jaan-dar janazon ko bhi mil jaaye mazar

Dost! Main dekh chuka Taj Mahal
. . . vapas chal

My friend, I have seen the Taj Mahal
    let us go back

A diamond boiling over with alabaster flowers
    Silvery minarets blazing in the fire of the moon
    Winking continuously at the poet's mind
    The grand and alluring mausoleum of an empress

Like a question, it flashed through the mind's eye
    The thought of those who lie in the streets like corpses
    Whose nerves and sinews shrink lifelessly
    Whose skulls smash like cymbals in the heat

My friend, I have seen the Taj Mahal
    let us go back

In this dome the beating heart of Shahjahan
    The smiling face of an empress on its walls
    Glittering from every layer satire and discrimination
    Over which history drapes the mask of love

I swear by the moonlight and by this world of wonders
    Like a canal of milk coming to the boil
    So too does this scene meets the traveller's gaze
    One who is reminded of the fate of Farhad

My friend, I have seen the Taj Mahal
    let us go back

This gleaming threshold, this becrowned dome
    It is these marvels that have encouraged the worship of graves

    Even the stars perforce bow in prostration
    Such is the boudoir of the much-adored empress

  Not a palace but a clearly visible division this is
      Like smoke on the face of life, like the dance of light on a grave
      Spreading across this garden tomb as soon as its hem shrinks
      May many life-filled funerals find such mausoleums

  My friend, I have seen the Taj Mahal
    let us go back

Kaifi joined the CPI in 1943 when he was twenty-four years old and remained a card-holding member his entire life. While the party suffered many ups and down in the course of its existence in India since its inception in 1925, its split in 1964 into the CPI and the CPI-M makes him write the hauntingly elegiac '*Awaara Sajdey*' that ends with this heart-breaking admission:

Eik ke baad Khuda eik chala aata thha
Keh diya aql ne tang aake Khuda koi nahiin

Gods would keep coming one after the other
Till finally, fed up, the brain said there's no God

Writing the introduction to his collected works, Kaifi begins thus: 'What I can say with conviction about myself is simply that I was born in subjugated India and grew old in independent India and will die in a socialist India. These are not the ravings of a lunatic nor the dream of a crazy idealist. My poetry and I have always been associated with socialism for which a great struggle has been going on for a long time in India and the world over. My poetry is born out of this very conviction.' Kaifi did not die in a socialist India and the Red Revolution that he and his fellow progressives had longed for and sung in many a passionate and rousing song never materialized. Perhaps it was this that made him cry out in anguish:

Koi to sood chukaye koi to zimma ley
Uss inquilab ka jo aaj tak udhaar sa hai

Someone should pay the interest, someone must own up
To that revolution that is still due till today

* * *

Love and romance run like warp through the woof of politics and protest in Kaifi's poetry. This collection chooses to focus on poems that reflect Kaifi's views on women and romance. As in all selections, this too is subjective. And, as in all things in a poet's life and career, there is growth and movement in Kaifi's portrayal of women. If there is an early poem such as '*Bewa ki Khudkushi*' ('A Widow's Suicide') and '*Doshiza Malan*' ('The Virginal Flower Girl'), there is also the powerful, stirring, anthem-like '*Aurat*' ('Woman') written while he is still a young man. Sweetly lyrical poems such as '*Pehla Salaam*' ('The First Greeting') and '*Andeshe*' ('Anxious Thoughts') or '*Pashemani*' (Regret') are juxtaposed with robust portrayals of womanhood in '*Behroopni*' ('She of the Many Faces') and '*Garbhwati*' ('The Pregnant Woman'). Taken together, they give a new meaning to the 'male gaze', how a man views women.

Translating Kaifi does not come without its share of perils. There is a *sangeetmayata*, a musicality, a sweet lyricism even in the most rousing of his poetry. There is also a completely idiosyncratic use of syntax, one that defies the conventions of prosody and a liberal use of the natural pauses that Urdu allows. All of this is enough to make an unwary translator trip over a seemingly simple nazm such as:

Tum pareshaan na ho baab-e-karam vaa na karo
Aur kuchh der pukaarungaa chala jaaungaa
Usii kuuche mein jahaan chaand ugaa karte hain
Shab-e-taariik guzaarungaa chala jaaungaa

Or this film lyric that sounds so haunting and poignant in the voice of Lata Mangeshkar:

Betaab dil ki tamanna yehi hai
Tumhey chaaheingey tumhey puujeingey
Tumhey apna Khuda banaeingey

A translation has been described as looking at the 'wrong' side of a carpet: the colour, sheen, pattern are all there; it's just that they are muted with none of the jewel-brightness and sharpness of the 'right' side facing up. I present this collection of Kaifi's nazms and lyrics to you with the full awareness of the inevitability of loss. Diminished though they are when they move from one language to another, especially from one language and its literary culture that is so disparate from the other, these translations will nevertheless, I hope, carry some trace of the brilliance of Kaifi's pen.

Rakhshanda Jalil
December 2018
New Delhi

POEMS

Shaukat ke Naam

Aisa jhonka bhi ik aaya thha ki dil bujhne laga thha
Tuune uss haal mein bhi mujh ko sambhale rakha
Kuchh andhere jo mere dum se miley thhe tujh ko
Afreen tujh ko ke naam unn ka ujaley rakha
Mere yeh sajde jo awara bhi badnaam bhi hain
Apni chaukhat pe saja le jo tere kaam ke hon

To Shaukat*

A gust had once come that made my heart sink
You kept me safe in that state too
The darkness that fell to your lot because of me
Bravo! You named it light
These prostrations of mine, both wayward and infamous
Deck your doorway with them if they are of some use to you

---

* Dedication to *Awaara Sajdey*

Pashemani

Main yeh soch kar uss ke dar se uthaa thha
Ki woh rok le gii manaa le gii mujh ko
Havaaon mein lahraataa aataa thha daaman
Ki daaman pakarh kar bithaa le gii mujh ko
Qadam aise andaaz se uth rahe thhe
Ki aavaaz de kar bulaa legi mujh ko

Magar us ne rokaa na mujh ko manaayaa
Na daaman hii pakrha na mujh ko bithaayaa
Na aawaaz hii di na mujh ko bulaayaa
Main aahista aahista barhhtaa hi aayaa
Yahaan tak ki uss se judaa ho gayaa main

Regret

I had left her doorway thinking
She would stop me, coax me to stay
The hem of my shirt billowing in the breeze
Made me hope she would hold it, make me sit
My steps rose and fell in such a manner
As though she would call out and stop me

But she neither stopped me, nor coaxed me to stay
Nor did she hold my hem and make me sit
She neither called out, nor summoned me back
I kept walking away slowly, ever so slowly
So much so that I was separated from her

Sarojini Naidu

Aziiz ma, meri hansmukh, meri bahaadur ma
Tamaam jauhar-e-fitrat jagaa diye tu ne
Mohabbat apne chaman se, gulon se, khaaron se
Mohabbaton ke khazaane lutaa diye tu ne

Banaa banaa ke mitaae gae nuqush-e-amal
Tire baġhair mukammal na ho sakii tasviir
Woh khvaab Jhansi ki rani ko jis ne chaunkayaa
Tira gihaad-e-musalsal usii ki hai taabiir

Usse hayaat ka sola-singaar kahte hain
Teri jabiin pe hain kuchh silvatein bhi tika bhi
Nazar mein jazb-e-yaqin dil mein soz-e-azaadi
Dahakta phuul bhi hai tu mahakta shola bhi

Zara zamin ko mehvar pe ghuum leney de
Yeh duniya tujh se tira soz-o-saaz maangegi
Jamaal sikhega khud-eitimadiyan tujh se
Hayaat-e-nau tire dil ka gudaaz maangegi

Sarojini Naidu

Dear mother, my cheerful, brave mother
You lit up all the jewels of nature
You loved your garden, its flowers and its thorns
You gave away vast treasures of love

Some of your activities were erased
But no picture could ever be complete without you
Your constant struggle illuminates the same dream
That had jolted the Rani of Jhansi awake

The wrinkles on your forehead and the tika
Augment the make-up and artistry of life
The fervour of belief in your gaze, the passion for freedom in
    your heart
You are both blazing flower and fragrant ember

Let the earth rotate on its axis
The world will ask for your fire and music
Beauty will learn self-confidence from you
New life will seek kindness from your heart

Behroopni

Ek gardan pe saikdon chehrey
Aur har chehrey par hazaaron daaġh
Aur har daaġh band darvaza
Raushni inn se aa nahin sakti
Raushni inn se ja nahin sakti

Tang siina hai hauz masjid ka
Dil woh dauna pujariyon ke baad
Chat-tey rahte hain jise kutte
Kutte dauna jo chaat lete hain
Devtaon ko kaat lete hain

Jaane kis kokh ne jana iss ko
Jaane kis sehn men javan hui
Jaane kis des se chali kam-baḳht
Vaise ye har zaban bolti hai
Zaḳhm khidki ki tarah kholti hai

Aur kahti hai jhank kar dil mein
Tera mazhab, tira aziim ḳhuda

She of the Many Faces

Hundreds of faces on one neck
And thousands of scars on each face
And every scar a closed door
That lets in no light
And lets out no light

The tank in the mosque is narrow-chested
The heart is a leaf plate that
Dogs keep licking away at
Once the pujaris are done
And then the dogs bite the gods

God knows which womb birthed her
God knows in which courtyard she grew
God knows which country the wretch came from
For she speaks in every tongue
And opens wounds as though they are windows

And then peering into the heart, she says
Your religion, your great God

Teri tahzib ke hasin sanam
Sab ko khatre ne aaj ghera hai
Baad un ke jahan andhera hai

Sard ho jaata hai lahu mera
Band ho jaati hain khuli ankhein
Aisa lagta hai jaise duniya mein
Sabhi dushman hain koi dost nahin
Mujh ko zinda nigal rahi hai zamin

Aisa lagta hai raakshas koi
Ek gaagar kamar men latka kar
Aasman par chadhega akhir-e-shab
Nuur saara nichod laega
Mere taare bhi tod laega

Yeh jo dharti ka phat gaya siina
Aur bahar nikal padey hain julus
Mujh se kahte hain tum hamare ho
Main agar inn ka huun to main kya huun
Main kisi ka nahin huun apna huun

Mujh ko tanhai ne diya hai janam
Mera sab kuchh akele-pan se hai
Kaun puchhega mujh ko mele mein
Saath jis din qadam badhaunga
Chaal main apni bhuul jaunga

Yeh aur aise hi chand aur saval
Dhundne par bhi aaj tak mujh ko
Jin ke ma baap ka mila na suragh
Zehn mein yeh undeil deti hai

The beautiful idols of your civilization
Danger engulfs everyone today
Darkness awaits the world after them

My blood runs cold
My open eyes shut
It seems as though everyone in the world is
An enemy and there are no friends
And the earth is swallowing me alive

It seems as though some ogre
A pitcher dangling from his waist
Will climb the sky before night ends
Squeeze out all the light
And snatch off my stars too

The earth's bosom has cracked open
And the processions that have burst out of it
Tell me that I am one of them
If I am theirs then who am I?
I am no one's; I am my own

I was birthed by solitude
All of me emanates from loneliness
Who will bother with me in a crowd?
The day I raise my feet in tandem with others
I will forget how to walk on my own

These and similar questions
Despite searching for them till this day
I have never found a trace of their parents
She pours these questions into my mind

Mujh ko mutthi mein bhench leti hai

Chahta huun ki qatl kar duun ise
Vaar lekin jab is pe karta huun
Mere siine pe zaḵhm ubharte hain
Mere maathe se ḵhuun tapakta hai
Jaane kya mera iss ka rishta hai

Andhiyon mein azaan di maine
Sankh phunka andheri raaton men
Ghar ke bahar saliib latkai
Ek ek dar se uss ko thukraya
Shahr se duur ja ke pheink aaya

Aur elaan kar diya ki utho
Barf si jam gai hai sinon mein
Garm boson se uss ko pighla do
Kar lo jo bhi gunah woh kam hai
Aaj ki raat jashn-e-adam hai

Yeh miri aastin se nikli
Rakh diya daud ke charaġh pe haath
Mal diya phir andhera chehre par
Hont se dil ki baat laut gaii
Dar tak aa ke baraat laut gaii

Uss ne mujh ko alag bula ke kaha
Aaj ki zindagi ka naam hai ḵhauf
Khauf hii who zamin hai jis mein
Firqe ugte hain firqe palte hain
Dhare sagar se kat ke chalte hain

She clenches me in her fist

I wish I could kill her
But when I strike her
Wounds break out on my breast
Blood drips from my forehead
God knows what binds me to her

I have given the call for prayer amidst storms
Sounded the conch on dark nights
Hung a crucifix outside my home
Made sure she was banished from every door
I discarded her far away from the city

And I announced: Arise!
Ice has formed on your chests
Melt it with hot kisses
Commit any sin you wish
Celebrate Adam tonight

She emerged from my sleeve
Snuffed out the lamp with her hand
Then rubbed the darkness on her face
Words rising from the heart turned back from the lips
The marriage party returned from the doorway

She took me aside and said:
Today, Fear is another name for Life
Fear is the soil in which
Sects grow and nourish
And streams are cut off from oceans

Khauf jab tak dilon men baaqi hai
Sirf chehra badalte rahna hai
Sirf lahja badalte rahna hai
Koi mujh ko mita nahin sakta
Jashn-e-adam mana nahin sakta

As long as the heart remains fearful
Only the face needs to change
Only the tone needs to change
No one can destroy me
No one can celebrate Adam

Andeshe

Ruuh bechain hai ik dil kii aziyyat kya hai
Dil hii shola hai to ye soz-e-mohabbat kya hai
Woh mujhe bhuul gaii iss kii shikayat kya hai
Ranj to ye hai ki ro ro ke bhulaayaa hogaa

Woh kahaan aur kahaan kahish-e-ġham, sozish-e-jaan
Uss kii rangiin nazar aur nuqush-e-hirmaan
Uss ka ehsaas-e-latiif aur shikast-e-armaan
Taana-zan ek zamaana nazar aayaa hogaa

Jhuk gaii hogii javaan-saal umangon kii jabiin
Mit gaii hogii lalak, duub gayaa hogaa yaqiin
Chhaa gayaa hogaa dhuaan, ghuum gaii hogii zamiin
Apne pahle hii gharaunde ko jo dhaayaa hogaa

Dil ne aise bhii kuchh afsaane sunaae honge
Ashk aankhon ne piye aur na bahaae honge
Band kamre mein jo ḳhat mere jalaae honge
Ek ek harf jabiin par ubhar aayaa hogaa

Anxious Thoughts

The spirit is restless what is the heart's torment
When the heart is aflame, to what avail this passion of love
Why complain if she has forgotten me
But the regret is that she must have cried while doing so

She and her pining and sorrow, and ardour for life
Her bright gaze and her disappointments engraved
Her delicate sensibilities and her vanquished hopes
How the world must have appeared like a taunt to her

How the forehead of youthful longings must have bowed
How her yearnings must have dried up, her faith doused
Mists must have enveloped her, and the earth spun on its axis
When she had to destroy her very first nest

Her heart must have told her just these sort of stories
Her eyes would have swallowed her tears, not letting a single
    drop fall
When she burned my letters behind closed doors
Every word must have appeared inscribed on her forehead

Uss ne ghabraa ke nazar laakh bachaaii hogii
Mit ke ik naqsh ne sau shakl dikhaaii hogii
Meiz se jab meri tasviir hataaii hogii
Har taraf mujh ko tadaptaa huaa paayaa hogaa

Be-mahal chhed pe jazbaat ubal aae honge
Gham pashemaan-e-tabassum mein dhal aae honge
Naam par mere jab aansu nikal aae honge
Sar na kaandhe se sahelii ke utthaayaa hogaa

Zulf zid kar ke kisii ne jo hataii hogii
Ruuthe jalvon pe khizaan aur bhii chhaaii hogii
Barq ashvon ne kaii din na giraaii hogii
Rang chehre pe kaii roz na aayaa hogaa

Flustered, she must have tried to evade every glance
Every fading inscription must have revealed a hundred faces
While removing my photograph from the table
She must have found me quivering in agony all around her

Inappropriately teased, her feelings must have boiled over
Her sorrows must have seeped into her abashed smile
When tears must have sprung up at the mention of my name
She wouldn't have raised her head from her friend's shoulder

When someone would have insisted on tidying her hair
Autumn would have spread in all its glory on her displeased
    beauty
Coquettish glances would not have flashed like lightning
And her face would have remained pale and colourless for days

Aurat

Utth meri jaan! mere saath hii chalna hai tujhe

Qalb-e-mahaul mein larzan sharar-e-jang hain aaj
Hausle waqt ke aur ziist ke yak-rang hain aaj
Abginon mein tapan walwala-e-sang hain aaj
Husn aur ishq hum-awaaz o hum-ahang hain aaj

Jis mein jalta huun usi aag mein jalna hai tujhe
Utth meri jaan! mere saath hii chalna hai tujhe

Tere qadmon mein hai firdaus-e-tamaddun kii bahaar
Teri nazron pe hai tahzib-o taraqqui ka madaar
Teri aaghosh hai gahwara-e-nafs-o-kirdaar
Taa-ba-kai gird tere wahm-o taayyun ka hisaar

Kaund kar majlis-e-khalwat se nikalana hai tujhe
Utth meri jaan! mere saath hii chalna hai tujhe

Tu ke be-jaan khilaunon se bahal jaati hai
Tapti saanson ki haraarat se pighal jaati hai

Woman

Arise, my love! You have to walk beside me

Sparks of war quiver in the air about us today
Time and life are equally audacious today
The heat in goblets equates the excitement in stone today
Beauty and love speak in the same voice and tone today

You too must burn in the fire I burn in
Arise, my love! You have to walk beside me

A spring of heavenly sophistication lies at your feet
Your gaze marks the limits of civilization and progress
Your embrace cradles the soul and character
Encircled by the fortress of your fears and fixations

You must dazzle your way out of this web of confinement
Arise, my dearest! You have to walk beside me

You who are mollified by lifeless toys
You who melt in the heat of feverish breaths

Paanv jis raah mein rakhti hai phisal jaati hai
Ban ke simaab har ik zarf mein dhal jaati hai

Ziist ke aahanii saanche mein bhii dhalnaa hai tujhe
Utth meri jaan mere saath hii chalna hai tujhe

Zindagi jehd mein hai sabr ke qaabu mein nahiin
Nabz-e-hasti ka lahu kaanpte aansu mein nahiin
Udne khulne mein hai nikhat kham-e-gesu mein nahiin
Jannat ik aur hai jo mard ke pahlu mein nahiin

Uss kii azaad ravish par bhii machalna hai tujhe
Utth meri jaan mere saath hii chalna hai tujhe

Goshe goshe mein sulagti hai chita tere liye
Farz ka bhes badalti hai qaza tere liye
Qahr hai teri har ik narm adaa tere liye
Zahr hii zahr hai duniya kii hawa tere liye

Rut badal daal agar phulna phalna hai tujhe
Utth meri jaan mere saath hii chalna hai tujhe

Qadr ab tak teri tariikh ne jaani hii nahiin
Tujh mein sholey bhii hai bas ashk-fishani hii nahiin
Tu haqiqat bhii hai dilchasp kahani hii nahiin
Teri hasti bhii hai ik chiiz jawani hii nahiin

Apni tariikh ka unwaan badalna hai tujhe
Utth meri jaan! mere saath hii chalna hai tujhe

Torh kar rasm ka but band-e-qadaamat se nikal
Zof-e-ishrat se nikal wahm-e-nazaakat se nikal

You who slip on the path on which you set foot
You who slide like mercury in every vessel

You must now pour yourself in the iron mould of life
Arise, my dearest! You have to walk beside me

Life lies in struggle, not in the thrall of patience
Quivering tears cannot contain the blood of pulsating life
Fragrance is in soaring and spreading, not in coiled tresses
There is another heaven too beyond a man's embrace

You must also frolic on its free pathways
Arise, my dearest! You have to walk beside me

Pyres smoulder for you in nooks and corners
Fate comes disguised as duty for you
Every soft gesture will rain wrath upon you
There is nothing but poison in the air for you

Change the season if you are to flower and flourish
Arise, my dearest! You have to walk beside me

History has still not acknowledged your worth
You contain sparks and not just tears
You are a reality and not just an interesting story
Your existence too is as real as your youth

You must change the title of your history
Arise, my dearest! You have to walk beside me

Break the idol of custom, step out of restrictions of conservatism
Cast aside the frailties of luxury and the whim of delicacy

Nafs ke khiinche hue halqa-e-azmat se nikal
Qaid ban jaae mohabbat to mohabbat se nikal

Raah ka khaar hii kya gul bhii kuchalna hai tujhe
Utth meri jaan! mere saath hii chalna hai tujhe

Torh ye azm-shikan daġhdaġha-e-pand bhii torh
Teri k̲h̲atir hai jo zanjir woh saugand bhii torh
Tauq ye bhii hai zamurrad ka gulu-band bhii torh
Torh paimana-e-mardaan-e-k̲h̲irad-mand bhii torh

Ban ke tufaan chhalakna hai ubalna hai tujhe
Utth meri jaan! mere saath hii chalna hai tujhe

Tu falatun o arastu hai tu zahra parvin
Tere qabze mein hai garduun teri thokar mein zamiin
Haan uttha jald uttha paa-e-muqaddar se jabiin
Main bhii rukne ka nahiin waqt bhii rukne ka nahiin

Larhkharhaegi kahaan tak ki sambhalnaa hai tujhe
Utth meri jaan! mere saath hii chalna hai tujhe

Walk out of the circle of honour drawn by the spirit
If love becomes a prison, break free of love too

Not just the thorn, you must crush the flower on your path
Arise, my dearest! You have to walk beside me

Break this crushing fortitude and this exultant moralizing
Break your own vows if they have turned into manacles
Break the necklace studded with precious stones if it has
      become a yoke
Break the goblet offered to you by men of wisdom and sagacity

Like a storm you must spill over and seethe
Arise, my dearest! You have to walk beside me

If you are Plato and Aristotle, you are also bright as the Pleiades
Heaven is in your control and earth lies beneath your feet
Raise your forehead, yes, raise it quickly, from the feet of destiny
I am not going to wait for you, neither will Time

How long will you stumble, you must take care
Arise, my dearest! You have to walk beside me

Bewa ki Khudkushi

Ye andheri raat ye saari fazaa soi hui
Patti patti manzar-e-ḳhaamosh mein khoi hui
Maujzan hai bahr-e-zulmat tiirgi ka josh hai
Shaam hii se aaj qindiil-e-falak ḳhaamosh hai
Chand taare hain bhi to be-nur pathraae hue
Jaise baasi haar mein hon phuul kumhlaae hue
Khap gayaa hai yuun ghataa mein chaandni ka saaf rang
Jis tarah maayusiyon mein dab ke rah jaae umang
Umdii hai kaali ghataa duniya duboney ke liye
Yaa chali hai baal khole raand roney ke liye
Jitni hai gunjaan basti utni hii viiraan hai
Har gali ḳhaamosh hai har raasta sunsaan hai
Ik makan se bhi makiin ki kuchh ḳhabar miltii nahiin
Chilmanein utthtii nahiin zanjiir-e-dar hiltii nahiin
So rahey hain mast-o-beḳhud ghar ke kul piir-o-javaan
Ho gaii hain band husn-o-ishq mein sargoshiyaan
Haan magar ik samt ik goshe mein koii nauhagar
Le rahii hai karvaton par karvatein dil thaam kar
Dil sambhaltaa hii nahin hai siina-e-sad-chaak mein
Phuul saa chehra ataa hai bevgii kii ḳhaak mein

48

A Widow's Suicide

This dark night when the entire world is fast asleep
When every leaf and twig is lost in the tableau of silence
The ocean of darkness is in turmoil and the gloom is filled with
    tumult
The lantern in the sky has been snuffed out since evening
The few stars that are about look lightless and dull
Like wilted flowers in a stale garland
The clear light of the moon is submersed in the clouds
Like enthusiasm that has been buried in disappointments
Are they dark clouds amassed to drown the world
Or is it a widow with open hair crying as she walks
The hamlet is as desolate as it is densely populated
Every alley is silent and every path deserted
No news emerges from those who inhabit these houses
The lattices are downed and chains bar the doors
All the old and young in the house are asleep and oblivious
Beauty and love have stopped whispering to each other
Yes, but there is a mourner in one distant corner
Tossing and turning on her bed, her heart sinking
A heart that won't stay in a breast with a hundred gashes

Ud chalii hai rang-e-ruḳh ban kar hayaat-e-musta.aar
Ho rahaa hai qalb-e-murda mein jawani ka fishaar
Hasratein dam todtii hain yaas kii aaġhosh mein
Saikdon shikve machalte hain lab-e-ḳhaamosh mein
Umr aamaada nahiin murda-parastii ke liye
Baar hai ye zinda mayyat dosh-e-hasti ke liye
Chaahti hai laakh qaabu dil pe paatii hii nahiin
Hai-re zaalim jawani bas mein aatii hii nahiin
Thartharaa kar girti hai jab suune bistar par nazar
Le ke ik karvat patak deti hai woh takiye pe sir
Jab khanak utthti hain sotii ladkiyon kii chudiyaan
Aah ban kar utthne lagtaa hai kaleje se dhuaan
Ho gai bewa ki ḳhaatir niind bhi jaise haraam
Muḳhtasar saa ahd-e-vaslat de gayaa soz-e-davaam
Dopahar ki chhaanv daur-e-shaadmaanii ho gayaa
Pyaas bhi bujhne na paai ḳhatm paani ho gayaa
Le rahi hai karvaton par karvatein baa-iztiraar
Aag mein paara hai yaa bistar pe jism-e-be-qaraar
Pad gaii ik aah kar ke ro ke utth baithii kabhi
Ungliyon mein le ke zulf-e-ḳham-ba-ḳham ainthi kabhi
Aa ke honthon par kabhii maayus aahein tham gaiin
Aur kabhi suuni kalaai par nigaahein jam gaiin
Itnii duniya mein kahiin apni jagah paati nahin
Yaas iss had kii ki shauhar kii bhii yaad aatii nahin
Aa rahey hain yaad paiham saas nandon ke suluk
Phat rahaa hai ġham se siina utth rahii hai dil mein huuk
Apni ma bahnon ka bhii aankhen churaanaa yaad hai
Aisi duniya mein kisi ka chhod jaanaa yaad hai
Byaaġhbaan to qabr mein hai kaun ab dekhe bahaar
Khud usii ko tiir us ke karne vaale hain shikar
Jab nazar aataa nahiin detaa koi bekas ka saath
Zahr ki shiishii ki jaanib ḳhud-ba-ḳhud badhtaa hai haath

A face like a flower is smeared with the ash of widowhood
The colour on her face gone like a frail life with a limited
    lifespan
The heart and soul of death hold her youth in its grasp
Unfulfilled desires die in the embrace of despair
A thousand reproaches quiver on her silent lips
Her years are not ready yet to worship the dead
This living corpse is a burden for a wronged life
No matter how hard she tries, she can't control her heart
When her trembling gaze falls on her desolate bed
Turning on her side she throws her head on the pillow
Her sighs rise like smoke from her singed heart
At the sudden tinkle of the bangles of girls asleep
As though even sleep is forbidden for a widow
A short-lived union has left an eternal fervour
A shade at the height of noon is now an era of happiness
The water ran out before the thirst could be slaked
Fretfully she tosses and turns on the bed
Her restless body like mercury in fire
Sometimes falls back with a sigh or sits up with a cry
The finger holding a curl of hair stiffens
The despondent sighs rising to her lips halt
And sometimes her glance falls on her bare wrists and freezes
She finds no place for herself in this big wide world
Such is her despair that she doesn't even remember her husband
All she recalls is how her mother-in-law and sister-in-law treat
    her
Her chest feels like bursting with grief with the pain shooting
    through her heart
She also remembers how her mother and sister avoid her
And how someone has left her behind in such a world
With the gardener in the grave, who will now tend to the spring?

Dil tadap kar kah rahaa hai jald iss duniya ko chhod
Chudiyaan todiin to phir zanjiir-e-hasti ko bhii tod
Dam agar niklaa to khoii zindagi mil jaaegii
Ye nahin to ḳhair tanhaa qabr hii mil jaaegii
Vaan tujhe zillat ki nazron se na dekhega koi
Chaahe hansnaa chaahe ronaa phir na rokegaa koi
Vaan sab ahl-e-dard hain sab saahab-e-insaaf hain
Rahbar aage jaa chuka raahein bhi teri saaf hain
Dil inhiin baaton mein uljhaa thaa ki dam ghabraa gaya
Haath le kar zahr ki shiishii labon tak aa gayaa
Tilmilaatii aankh jhapkatii jhijaktii haanptii
Pii gaii kul zahr aaḳhir thartharaatii kanptii
Maut ne jhatka diyaa kul uzv dhiile ho gae
Saans ukhdii, nabz dubii, hont niile ho gae
Aankh jhapkii ashk tapka hichkii aaii kho gaii
Maut ki aaġhosh mein ik aah bhar kar so gaii

Aur kar ik aah sulge hind ki rasmon ka daam
Ai javaana-marg bewa tujh pe Kaifi ka salaam

Her own arrows will be used to hunt her down
The hand reaches for the bottle of poison on its own
When no one comes forward to help the helpless
And the heart, agitated, cries out, urging her to leave this world
    at the earliest
If you have broken your bangles, break this chain of life too
Only when your breath leaves you, will you find your lost
    existence
If not that, at least you will find a solitary grave
Where no one will look at you with wounding eyes
No one will stop you from laughing or crying as you please
Where everyone has known suffering and loves justice
Your guide has gone on ahead and the path before you is clear
Entangled in these thoughts, her breathing becomes shallow
And her hand brings the bottle of poison to her lips
Irritably blinking her eyes, uncertain and gasping for breath
She drinks all the poison, trembling and shivering
Her limbs fall loose at death's mighty heave
Her breath leaves her, her pulse drops, her lips turn blue
Her eyes droop, a tear falls, she hiccups and is gone
With a sigh she goes to sleep in the embrace of death

Sigh once more so that the noose of Hind's customs goes up in
    flames
Kaifi salutes the death of a young widow

Doshiza Malan

Lo pau phatii woh chhup gaii taaron ki anjuman
Lo jaam-e-mahr se woh chhalakne lagi kiran
Khichne laga nigaah mein fitrat ka baankpan
Jalve zamiin pe barse zamiin ban gaii dulhan

Guuunje taraane subh ka ik shor ho gaya
Aalam mai-e-baqaa mein sharaabor ho gaya

Phulii shafaq fazaa mein hina tilmilaa gaii
Ik mauj-e-rang kaanp ke aalam pe chhaa gaii
Kul chaandni simat ke gulon mein samaa gaii
Zarre bane nujum zamin jagmagaa gaii

Chhodaa sahar ne tiirgi-e-shab ko kaat ke
Udne lagi hawa mein kiran ose chaat ke

Machli jabiin-e-sharq pe iss tarah mauj-e-nuur
Lahraa ke tairne lagi aalam mein barq-e-tuur

The Virginal Flower Girl

Look! Dawn has broken and the assembly of stars has gone into
    hiding
Look! A beam of light spills from the goblet of the sun
An impish beauty begins to appear in nature
Luminous light begins to rain down and the earth turns into a
    bride

Songs of the morning begin to echo and a tumult breaks out
The universe is drenched in the wine of immortality

The rose-tinted twilight makes the henna leaves quake
A wave of colour quivers and courses through the universe
Moonlight gathers itself and seeps into flowers
Specks turn into stars and the earth begins to sparkle

But as dawn cuts through the darkness of the night
A beam of light dances on, licking a drop of dew

A wave of light trembles on the forehead of the rising sun
As though lightning from Mount Sinai ripples across the sky

Udne lagi shamiim chhalakne laga suruur
Khilne lage shagufe chahakne lage tuyuur

Jhonkey chaley hawa ke shajar jhumne lagey
Masti mein phuul kanton ka munh chuumne lagey

Tham tham ke zau-fishaan hua zarron pe aaftaab
Chhidka hawa ne sabza-e-k̲hvaabiida par gulaab
Murjhaaii pattiyon mein machalne laga shabaab
Larzish hui gulon ko barasne lagii sharaab

Rindaan-e-mast aur bhi sarmast ho gaey
Tharraa ke hont jaam mein paivast ho gaey

Doshiza ek k̲hush-qad o k̲hush-rang-o-k̲huub-ru
Maalan ki nuur-diida gulistaan ki aabru
Mahka rahi hai phulon se daamaan-e-aarzu
Tiflii liye hai gode mein tufaan-e-rang-o-bu

Rangiiniyon mein khelii gulon mein palii huii
Nauras kalii mein qaus-e-quzah hai dhalii huii

Masti mein ruk̲h pe baal pareshaan kiye hue
Baadal mein sham-e-tuur farozaan kiye hue
Har samt naqsh-e-paa se charaag̲haan kiye hue
Aanchal ko baar-e-gul se gulistaan kiye hue

Lahraa rahii hai baad-e-sahar paanv chuum ke
Phirtii hai tiitarii sii g̲hazab jhuum jhuum ke

A fragrance wafts through and intoxication brims over
Buds bloom just as birds begin to chirp and chirrup

Trees sway and bow to gentle puffs of breeze
Heady flowers kiss the mouth of thorns

Bit by bit the sun begins to irradiate specks and particles
The air sprinkles rose water on the somnolent greenery
Youth ripples anew in wilted leaves
A quiver runs through flowers and wine begins to rain

Intoxicated drinkers become even more intoxicated
With a frisson lips fasten to the goblet's brim

The virginal girl, beautiful, fair, tall
This light-giving flower girl, the pride of the garden
Filling her hem of hopes with flowers
In her lap this child carries a storm of colours and aromas

Playing amid colours and growing up among flowers
She is a bud suffused with the colours of the rainbow

In gay abandon her face covered by scattered tresses
Like the light from Sinai gleaming through clouds
Like lamps, her footprints light up paths in every direction
Her hem heavy with flowers she has turned into a garden herself

The morning breeze billows about, kissing her feet
Like a partridge she flits, swaying in a mad frenzy

Zulfon mein taab-e-sumbul-e-pechaan liye hue
Aariz mein shokh rang-e-gulistaan liye hue
Aankhon mein ruh-e-baada-e-irfaan liye hue
Honthon mein aab-e-laal-e-badakhshaan liye hue

Fitrat ne tol tol ke chashm-e-qubul mein
Saaraa chaman nichod diyaa ek phuul mein

Ai huur-e-baaġh itnii khudii se na kaam le
Ud kar shamiim-e-gul kahiin aanchal na thaam le
Kaliyon ka le payaam sahar ka salaam le
Kaifi se husn-e-dost ka taaza kalaam le

Shaaer ka dil hai muft mein kyuun dard-mand ho
Ik gul idhar bhi nazm agar ye pasand ho

In the coils of her hair she carries the lustre of the sumbul*
In her cheeks all the bright colours of the garden
In her eyes the essence of a sweeping knowledge
On her lips the clouds of gems and rubies

Nature has measured out and poured into her accepting eyes
And squeezed the entire garden into one flower

O celestial nymph of the garden, beware of pride
Lest the flower's billowing fragrance fly up and catch your hem
Heed the message of the buds, receive the salutation of the
   dawn
From Kaifi accept the latest verses on the beauty of a friend

It is a poet's heart, why should it be needlessly empathetic?
Give me a flower too if you like this poem of mine

---

* A sweetly scented spikenard, to which the Persians compare the
locks of a mistress

Ek Dua

Ab aur kya tira biimaar baap degaa tujhe
Bas ik dua ki k̲hudaa tujh ko kamyaab karey
Woh taank de tire aanchal mein chaand aur taare
Tu apne vaaste jis ko bhi intik̲haab karey

A Prayer

What else can your ailing father give you
Except a prayer that God grant you success
And may the one you choose for yourself
Stitch on your hem both moon and the stars

Ek Bosa

Jab bhi chuum leta huun un hasiin aankhon ko
Sau charaaġh andhere mein jhilmilaane lagte hain

Khushk ḳhushk honthon mein jaise dil khinch aataa hai
Dil mein kitne aaiine thartharaane lagte hain

Phuul kya shagufe kya chaand kya sitaare kya
Sab raqiib qadmon par sar jhukaane lagte hain

Zehn jaag utthtaa hai ruuh jaag utthtii hai
Naqsh aadmiyat ke jagmagaane lagte hain

Lau nikalne lagti hai mandiron ke siine se
Devtaa fazaaon mein muskuraane lagte hain

Raqs karne lagtii hain muratein Ajantaa kii
Muddaton ke lab-basta ġhaar gaane lagte hain

Phuul khilne lagte hain ujde ujde gulshan mein
Tishna tishna giitii par abr chhaane lagte hain

A Kiss

Whenever I kiss these beautiful eyes
A hundred lamps begin to glimmer in the darkness

My heart gets drawn to my dry lips
And countless mirrors begin to shimmer

Not just flowers and buds but the stars and the moon
All my rivals begin to bow down at my feet

My mind wakes up and my spirit awakens too
Imprints of humanity begin to shine brightly

Incandescent desires arise from the bosom of temples
Gods begin to smile around me

The statues of Ajanta begin to dance
Their lips sealed for centuries, caves begin to sing

Flowers begin to bloom in desolate gardens
Clouds begin to gather over the thirsting earth

Lamha bhar ko ye duniya zulm chhod detii hai
Lamha bhar ko sab patthar muskuraane lagte hain

For a moment the earth forsakes its cruelties
For a moment all the rocks begin to smile

Ek Lamha!

Zindagi naam hai kuchh lamhon ka
Aur un mein bhi vahii ik lamha
Jis mein do boltii aankhein
Chaai ki pyaalii se jab utthiin
To dil mein dubiin
Duub ke dil mein kahiin
Aaj tum kuchh na kaho
Aaj main kuchh na kahuun
Bas yunhii baithe raho
Haath mein haath liye
Gham ki sauġhaat liye
Garmi-e-jazbaat liye
Kaun jaane ki usii lamhe mein
Duur parbat pe kahiin
Barf pighalne hii lagey

A Moment!

Life is nothing but a few moments
And among those, that one moment
When two eloquent eyes
Rise from the cup of tea
And drown in my heart
And doing so, they say:
Don't say anything today
And I won't either
Let's just sit here like this
Holding each other's hand
Cradling the gift of sadness
Nurturing the heat of passions
Who knows in this very moment
In some faraway mountain
The ice might just begin to thaw

Ehtiyat

Ab tum aaġhosh-e-tasawur mein bhi aayaa na karo
Mujh se bikhre hue gesu nahiin dekhe jaate
Surḳh aankhon ki qasam kaanpti palkon ki qasam
Thartharaate hue aansu nahiin dekhe jaate

Ab tum aaġhosh-e-tasawur mein bhi aayaa na karo
Chhut jaane do jo daamaan-e-vafaa chhut gayaa
Kyuun ye laġhziida-ḳhiraamii pe pashiimaan-nazarii
Tum ne todaa to nahiin rishta-e-dil tuut gayaa

Ab tum aaġhosh-e-tasawur mein bhi aayaa na karo
Merii aahon se ye ruḳhsaar na kumhlaa jaaen
Dhundtii hogii tumhein ras mein nahaaii huii raat
Jaao kaliyaan na kahiin sej ki murjhaa jaaen

Ab tum aaġhosh-e-tasawur mein bhi aayaa na karo
Main iss ujdey huwe pehlu mein bitha loon na kahiin
Lab-e shiriin ka namak aariz-e namkiin ki mithas
Apne tarsey huwe honton mein chura loon na kahiin

Caution

Don't come now, not even in the embrace of my imagination
I cannot bear to see your hair in such disarray
I swear by your red eyes and your quivering lashes
I cannot bear to see these trembling tears

Don't come now, not even in the embrace of my imagination
Let go of the hem of fidelity that remains
Why these regretful glances at that trembling walk
You didn't break the bond of the heart; it broke

Don't come now, not even in the embrace of my imagination
Lest these cheeks wilt in the heat of my sighs
The night bathed in nectar must be searching for you
Go, lest the buds on the bed wither away

Don't come now, not even in the embrace of my imagination
Lest I make you sit down beside my desolate side
And steal the salt of these sweet lips and the sweetness of salty
    cheeks
With my yearning thirsting lips

Ab tum aaġhosh-e-tasawur mein bhi aayaa na karo
Tum ko yeh rasm bhi duniya na nibhaane degii
Badh ke daaman se lipat jaayegi yuun taaza bahaar
Meri aaghosh-e tasawur mein na aane degii

Don't come now, not even in the embrace of my imagination
For this world will not let you follow this custom
And the fresh spring will reach out to embrace you
And not let you come to me, not even in the embrace of my
    imagination

Naya Husn

Kitnii rangiin hai fazaa kitnii hasiin hai duniya
Kitnaa sarshaar hai zauq-e-chaman-aaraaii aaj
Iss saliiqe se sajaaii gaii bazm-e-giitii
Tu bhi diivaar-e-Ajanta se utar aaii aaj

Ru-numaaii ki ye saa.at ye tahii-dastii-e-shauq
Na churaa sakta huun aankhein na milaa sakta huun
Pyaar sauġhaat, vafa nazr, mohabbat tohfa
Yahi daulat tire qadmon pe lutaa sakta huun

Kab se taḳhiil mein larzaan thaa ye naazuk paikar
Kab se ḳhvaabon mein machalti thii jawani teri
Mere afsaane ka unvaan banii jaati hai
Dhal ke saanche mein haqiqat ki kahani teri

Marhale jhel ke nikhraa hai mazaaq-e-taḳhliiq
Sa.ii-e-paiham ne diye hain ye ḳhad-o-ḳhaal tujhe
Zindagi chaltii rahii kanton pe, angaaron par
Jab milii itnii hasiin, itnii subuk chaal tujhe

New Beauty

How colourful is the ambience, how beautiful the world
How intoxicating the taste for adorning the garden today
The universe has been assembled with such grace
And you too have stepped off the walls of Ajanta

This moment of seeing your face and my own inadequate passion
I can neither steal my gaze away nor meet yours
The gift of love, the offer of fidelity, the present of passion
That's all the wealth I can lay at your feet

For long has this delicate form been quivering in my imagination
For long has your youth been tumultuously alive in my dreams
Cast in the mould of reality
Your story is becoming the title of mine

Taste and creativity have attained perfection evolving through
    stages
Constant effort has given you this form and feature
Life kept walking on many thorns and embers
Before this beautiful, this nimble a gait became yours

Tere qaamat mein hai insaan ki bulandi ka vaqaar
Dukhtar-e-shahr hai, tahzib ka shahkaar hai tu
Ab na jhapkegii palak, ab na hatengii nazrein
Husn ka mere liye aakhirii me.aar hai tu

Ye tiraa paikar-e-siimiin, ye gulaabi sari
Dast-e-mehnat ne shafaq ban ke udhaa dii tujh ko
Jis se mahruum hai fitrat ka jamaal-e-rangiin
Tarbiyat ne vo lataafat bhi sikhaa dii tujh ko

Aagahii ne teri baaton mein khilaaiin kaliyaan
Ilm ne shakkariin lahje mein nichode anguur
Dilrubaaii ka ye andaaz kise aataa thaa
Tu hai jis saans mein nazdiik usii saans mein duur

Ye lataafat, ye nazaakat, ye hayaa, ye shokhii
Sau diye jalte hain umdii hui zulmat ke khilaaf
Lab-e-shaadaab pe chhalkii hui gulnaar hansii
Ik baghaavat hai ye aaiin-e-jaraahat ke khilaaf

Hausle jaag utthe soz-e-yaqiin jaag utthaa
Nigah-e-naaz ke be-naam ishaaron ko salaam
Tu jahaan rahtii hai us arz-e-hasiin par sajda
Jin mein tu miltii hai un raah-guzaaron ko salaam

Aa qariib aa ki ye juudaa main pareshaan kar duun
Tishna-kamii ko ghataaon ka payaam aa jaae
Jis ke maathe se ubhartii hain hazaaron subhein
Meri duniya mein bhi aisi koi shaam aa jaae

Your height has the loftiness of Man's dignity
You are the daughter of the city, the masterpiece of civilization
My eyes will not blink now, nor will my gaze rove
This is the ultimate standard of beauty for me

This silvery form of yours, this rose-coloured sari
Twilight has draped it upon you with its own diligent hand
Your upbringing has rendered you the vivid beauty,
The exquisiteness of which even nature is bereft of

Your discernment makes flowers bloom when you speak
And knowledge makes grapes squeeze their sweetness in your
    voice
Who else possesses this alluring art of drawing one's heart
For the very breath that draws you closer moves you farther

This elegance, this delicacy, this bashfulness, this coquetry
Like a hundred lamps burning against a swelling sea of darkness
Laughter the colour of pomegranate flowers spilling on
    blooming lips
Is a rebellion against the rules of surgery

Courage has awakened, the passion of belief has woken
I salute the nameless gestures of the glance of love
I prostrate before that beautiful land where you live
I salute the paths you tread

Come, come close to me that I may push your coiled hair in
    disarray
That thirst may get the message of rain-bearing clouds
The forehead from which a thousand mornings burst forth
If only such an evening would come into my world too

Nazrana

Tum pareshaan na ho, baab-e-karam vaa na karo
Aur kuchh deir pukarungaa chalaa jaaungaa
Usii kuuche mein jahaan chaand ugaa karte hain
Shab-e-taariik guzaarungaa, chalaa jaaungaa

Raasta bhuul gayaa, yaa yahii manzil hai meri
Koi laayaa hai ki khud aayaa huun maalum nahiin
Kahte hain husn ki nazrein bhi hasiin hotii hain
Main bhi kuchh laayaa huun, kya laayaa huun maalum nahiin

Yuun to jo kuchh thaa mere paas main sab bech aayaa
Kahiin inaam milaa, aur kahiin qiimat bhii nahiin
Kuchh tumhaare liye aankhon mein chhupaa rakkhaa hai
Dekh lo aur na dekho to shikayat bhi nahiin

Ek to itnii hasiin dusre ye aaraaish
Jo nazar padtii hai chehre pe thhahar jaati hai
Muskura deti ho rasman bhi agar mahfil mein
kI dhanak tuut ke siinon mein bikhar jaati hai

Tribute

Don't be troubled, don't open the door of kindness
I will call out to you a while longer, then leave
In that narrow lane where moons are said to grow
I will spend the dark night, then go away

Have I forgotten my way, or is this my destination
I don't know if I have been brought here or have come on my
    own
They say even the glances of beauty are beautiful
I too have brought something; I don't know what

Though I have come away selling whatever I had with me
For some I was rewarded, for some I didn't even get a fair price
Some I have hidden away for you in my eyes
Take a look, but I shall have no complaints even if you don't

For one, you are so beautiful; and, so well adorned too
The glance that falls on your face stops and stays there
Even if you smile formally in a gathering
Fragments of the rainbow scatter in many a breast

Garm boson se taraashaa huaa naazuk paikar
Jis kii ik aanch se har ruuh pighal jaati hai
Maine sochaa hai ki sab sochte honge shaayad
Pyaas iss tarah bhi kya saanche mein dhal jaati hai

Kya kamii hai jo karogi miraa nazraana qubuul
Chaahne vaale bahut, chaah ke afsaane bahut
Ek hii raat sahii garmii-e-hangaama-e-ishq
Ek hii raat mein jal marte hain parvaane bahut

Phir bhi ik raat mein sau tarah ke morh aate hain
Kaash tum ko kabhi tanhaaii ka ehsaas na ho
Kaash aisaa na ho ghere rahe duniya tum ko
Aur iss tarah ki jis tarah koi paas na ho

Aaj ki raat jo meri hii tarah tanhaa hai
Main kisi tarah guzaarungaa chalaa jaaungaa
Tum pareshaan na ho, baab-e-karam vaa na karo
Aur kuchh deir pukarungaa chalaa jaaungaa

This delicate form chiselled with hot kisses
Every single flame of which serves to melt a soul
If I have thought of it, everyone else must have too:
Can thirst ever be moulded like this?

What do you lack that you should accept my tribute
There are many who love you and countless their stories of love
Only one night is enough for the heat and passion of love
Many a moth singes and dies in that one night

Yet, a night can entail a hundred twists and turns
May you never experience that sense of loneliness
May the world never crowd around you
Nor that there be no one beside you

The night that is as lonely as I am
I will pass it somehow and leave
Don't be troubled, don't open the door of kindness
I will call out to you a while longer, then go away

Pyar ka Jashn

Pyaar ka jashn nai tarah manaanaa hogaa
Gham kisi dil mein sahi ġham ko mitaanaa hogaa

Kaanpte honthon pe paimaan-e-vafaa kyaa kahnaa
Tujh ko laai hai kahaan laġhzish-e-paa kyaa kahnaa
Mere ghar mein tire mukhde ki ziyaa kyaa kahnaa
Aaj har ghar kaa diyaa mujh ko jalaanaa hogaa

Ruuh chehron pe dhuaan dekh ke sharmaati hai
Jhenpi jhenpi si mire lab pe hansi aati hai
Tere milne ki ḳhushi dard bani jaati hai
Hum ko hansnaa hai to auron ko hansaanaa hogaa

Soi soi hui aaankhon mein chhalakte hue jaam
Khoi khoi hui nazron mein mohabbat ka payaam
Lab shirin pe miri tishna-labi kaa inaam
Jaane inaam milegaa ki churaanaa hogaa

Meri gardan mein tiri sandali baahon ka ye haar
Abhi aansu thhe in aankhon mein abhi itnaa ḳhumaar

A Celebration of Love

The festival of love must be celebrated in a new way
Sadness must be erased from every heart

The vow of loyalty on tremulous lips is a sight indeed
See how far your trembling feet have brought you indeed
Your luminous face in my home is a sight indeed
But today I must light the lamp in every home too

The spirit shies away from the smoke on the faces
Abashed and shamefaced a smile reaches my lips
The pleasure of meeting you turns into pain
If we laugh we must make others laugh too

The goblets brimming over from half-sleeping eyes
The message of love in those bemused lost glances
The reward for my thirsting lips on those sweet lips
Will it be given or will I need to steal it?

This garland of sandalwood-scented arms around my neck
Tears in these eyes a moment ago, now this headiness

Main na kahtaa thaa mire ghar mein bhi aaegi bahaar
Shart itni thi ki pahle tujhe aanaa hogaa

Did I not say that spring would come to my home too
The only condition being that first you should come

Tasawur

Yeh kis tarah yaad aa rahii ho ye k̲h̲vaab kaisaa dikhaa rahii ho
Ki jaise sach-much nigaah ke saamne khadii muskuraa rahii ho
Ye jism-e-naazuk, ye narm baahein, hasiin gardan, sudaul baazu
Shagufta chehra, saloni rangat, ghaneraa judaa, siyaah gesu
Nashiilii aankhein, rasiilii chitvan, daraaz palkein, mahiin abru
Tamaam shok̲h̲i, tamaam bijli, tamaam masti, tamaam jaadu

Hazaaron jaadu jagaa rahii ho
Yeh k̲h̲vaab kaisaa dikhaa rahii ho

Gulaabi lab, muskuraate aariz, jabiin kushaada, buland qaamat
Nigaah mein bijliyon kii jhil-mil, adaaon mein shabnamii
    lataafat
Dhadaktaa siina, mahaktii saansein, navaa mein ras, ankhdiyon
    mein amrit
Hama halaavat, hama malaahat, hama tarannum, hama nazaakat

Lachak lachak gungunaa rahi ho
Yeh k̲h̲vaab kaisaa dikhaa rahii ho

Imagination

Why do I remember you thus, what is this dream you show
As though you are standing in front of me, smiling
This delicate body, the soft hands, this beautiful neck, these
supple arms
This cheerful face, the dusky complexion, this thick bun, the
dark tresses
The intoxicating eyes, the luscious form, the long eyelashes, the
delicate brows
All the mischief, all the lightning, all the coquetry, all the
magical charm

You bring to life a thousand spells
What is this dream you show

Pink lips, smiling cheeks, high forehead, tall stature
Flashes of lightning in the glance, a dewy delicacy in the manners
Throbbing breast, fragrant breaths, ambrosia in the air, nectar
in the eyes
Every sweetness, all piquancy, every melody, all delicate grace

To kya mujhe tum jalaa hii logii galey se apne lagaa hii logii
Jo phuul juude se gir padaa hai tadap ke uss ko utthaa hii logii
Bhadakte sholon, kadaktii bijlii se mera ḳhirman bachaa hii
    logii
Ghaneri zulfon ki chhaanv mein muskuraa ke mujh ko chhupaa
    hii logii

Ki aaj tak aazmaa rahii ho
Yeh ḳhvaab kaisaa dikhaa rahii ho

Nahiin mohabbat ki koi qiimat jo koi qiimat adaa karogii
Vafaa ki fursat na degii duniya hazaar azm-e-vafaa karogii
Mujhe bahalne do ranj-o-ġham se sahaare kab tak diyaa karogii
Junun ko itnaa na gudgudaao, pakad luun daaman to kya karogii

Qariib badhtii hii aa rahii ho
Yeh ḳhvaab kaisaa dikhaa rahii ho

You hum, swaying softly
What is this dream you show

So will you singe me then, will you embrace me
Anguished, will you pick up the flower that has fallen from your
    hair
Will you save my harvest from the flaring sparks and crackling
    thunder
Will you smile and hide me in the shade of your dense locks

For you have been testing me all along
What is this dream you show

There is no price for love, so there's none for you to pay
Despite all your vows of fidelity, the world will not give you
    time
Let me pacify myself with my griefs and sorrows; how long will
    you support me
Don't tease my passions, for what will you do if I catch you by
    your hem

You come closer and closer still
What is this dream you show

Tum

Shaguftagi ka lataafat ka shaahkar ho tum
Faqat bahaar nahiin haasil-e-bahaar ho tum
Jo ek phuul mein hai qaid vo gulistaan ho
Jo ik kalii mein hai pinhaan vo laala-zaar ho tum
Halaavaton kii tamannaa, malaahaton kii muraad
Ghurur kaliyon ka phulon ka inkisaar ho tum
Jise tarang mein fitrat ne gungunaayaa hai
Vo Bhairvi ho, vo Deepak ho vo Malhaar ho tum
Tumhaare jism mein khvaabiida hain hazaaron raag
Nigaah chhedtii hai jis ko vo sitaar ho tum
Jise utthaa na sakii justuju vo moti ho
Jise na gundh sakii aarzu vo haar ho tum
Jise na buujh saka ishq vo pahelii ho
Jise samajh na saka pyaar bhi vo pyaar ho tum
Khudaa karey kisii daaman mein jazb ho na sakein
Ye mere ashk-e-hasiin jin se aashkaar ho tum

You

You are the epitome of cheerfulness and elegance
Not just the spring, you are the product of springtime
You are the garden captive in a single flower
You are the bed of roses concealed in a single bud
The yearning for sweetness, the desire for piquancy
You are the haughtiness of buds, the modesty of flowers
You are the Bhairavi, the Deepak, the Malhar
That Nature has hummed melodiously
A thousand ragas dream inside your body
You are the sitar whose strings are plucked by a gaze
You are the pearl that longing cannot pluck
You are the garland that yearning cannot weave
You are the riddle that love cannot solve
You are the love that even love cannot understand
May these beautiful tears of mine, god willing,
Never find a hem to soak them

Ajnabi

Ai hama-rang hama-nur hama-soz-o-gudaaz
Bbazm-e-mahtaab se aane ki zarurat kyaa thi
Tu jahaan thin usin jannat men nikhartaa tiraa ruup
Is jahannam ko basaane ki zarurat kyaa thi

Ye khad-o-khaal ye khvaabon se taraashaa huaa jism
Aur dil jis pe khad-o-khaal kin narmin bhin nisaar
Khaar hin khaar sharaare hin sharaare hain yahaan
Aur tham tham ke uthaa paanv bahaaron kin bahaar

Tishnagin zahr bhin pin jaatin hai amrit kin tarah
Jaane kis jaam pe ruk jaa.e nigaah-e-ma.asum
Dubte dekhaa hai jin aankhon men mai-khaana bhin
Pyaas un aankhon kin bujhe yaa na bujhe kyaa ma.alum

Hain sabhin husn-parast ahl-e-nazar saahib-e-dil
Koin ghar men koin mahfil men sajaa.egaa tujhe
Tu faqat jism nahinn sher bhin hai giit bhin hai
Kaun ashkon kin ghanin chhaanv men gaa.egaa tujhe

Stranger

You who are full of colours, filled with light, and passion and
    tenderness
Why did you leave the moon's banquet?
Your beauty would have been enhanced in the heaven you
    lived in
Why did you come to live in this hell?

This form and features, this body chiselled from dreams
And a heart way superior to the form and features
There is nothing here, but thorns and flares
Pick your way slowly, O choicest spring of all springs

Thirst is known to gulp poison as though it is nectar
Who knows on which chalice the innocent gaze will rest?
The eyes in which I have seen taverns drown
Will their thirst ever be assuaged?

Everyone here loves beauty, a connoisseur of impeccable taste
Someone will adorn you in their home, others in gatherings of
    friends

Tujh se ik dard kaa rishta bhin hai bas pyaar nahinn
Apne aanchal pe mujhe ashk bahaa lene de
Tu jahaan jaatin hai jaa, rokne vaalaa main kaun
Apne raaste men magar sham.a jalaa lene de

You are not merely a body; you are a verse, and a poem too
Who will hum you in the dense shade of tears

It's not love alone that binds us but sorrows too
Let me shed my tears on your veil
Go, wherever you wish; who am I to stop you
But let me light candles along the path you take

Pehla Salaam

Eik chanchal jhijhak, eik alharh payaam
Hai 'Kaifi' kisi ka woh pehla salaam

Phool rukhsaar ke rasmasane lagey
Haath uththa qadam dagmagane lagey

Rang sa khaal-o khad se jhalakne laga
Sar se rangiin aanchal dhalakne laga

Ajnabiyat aankhein churaane lagii
Dil dhadakne lagai, lehar aane lagii

Saans mein ik gulabi girah parh gayii
Hont tharray, simtey, nazar garh gayii

Reh gaya umr bhar ke liye yeh hijaab
Kyun na sambhla hua de saka main jawaab

Kyun main be-qasd, be-azm, be-waasta
Doosri simt ghabra ke takne laga

The First Greeting

A playful hesitation, an innocent message
Such, Kaifi, was that certain someone's first greeting

The flowers on her cheeks were drenched
As her hand rose and her steps faltered

A colour began to spill from her body
As the veil began to slip from her head

The sense of unfamiliarity became a stranger
As the heart beat amidst rising waves

The breath tied itself in rose-hued knots
Lips trembled, grew still, the gaze held steadfast

This misgiving I will carry all my life
Why did my response lack poise

Flustered, why did I suddenly, thoughtlessly, needlessly
Begin to look in the other direction

Aaina

Aaina torh diya, torh diya, torh diya
Shakl eik baar zara dekh to lo
Dekho, ab kaisi nazar aati ho
Phir wahi ankhon mein rang aata hai
Ya jhijhal jaati hai, dar jaata hai

Isi aaine mein dekha thha woh husn
Jiska dushwaar yaquin hota hai
Aur poochha thha bade naaz ke saath
Koi itna bhi hasiin hota hai

Isme aaine ki khuubi to nahin
Husn hab thha to nazar aaya thha
Paa chuki thhi tumhe duniya lekin
Tumne apne ko kahaan paya thha

Aur jab apne ko paaya tumne
Jaane aaine ko kyon torh diya
Haadsa yeh bhi nahi hai lekin

Mirror

You have broken the mirror, smashed it, shattered it!
See your face but once
See how you look now
Does that same colour seep into your eyes
Or do you turn bashful, and get scared

I had seen a beauty in this very mirror
One that is hard to believe
And had asked with great pride:
Can anyone be so beautiful?

There was nothing special about the mirror
It was the beauty that made it so
The world had discovered you even though
You were yet to find yourself

And when you finally found yourself
Who knows why you broke the mirror
That in itself was not such a calamity

Dekhna apne ko kya chhorh diya

Shakl eik baar zara dekh to lo
Dekho, ab kaisi nazar aati ho

But that you stopped looking at yourself

See your face, but once
See, how you look now

Akhfa-i Muhabbat

Tum muhabbat ko chhupatii kyun ho?

Hai! Yeh jabr ki soorat jiina
Mooh bigaarhe huwe amrit piina
Kaanpti rooh dhadakta siina

Jurm fitrat ko banatii kyun ho?
Tum muhabbat ko chhupatii kyun ho?

Dil bhi hai dil mein tamanna bhi hai
Kuchh jawaani ka taqaaza bhi hai
Tum ko apne par bharosa bhi hai

Jheinp kar aankh milatii kyun ho?
Tum muhabbat ko chhupatii kyun ho?

Haan woh hanstein hain jo insaan nahiin
Jinko kuchh ishq ka irfan nahiin
Sang zaadon mein zara jaan nahiin

Concealing Love

Why do you hide your love?

Oh, to live this life of tyranny
Oh! To love like this in fear
Drinking nectar with a twisted face
Trembling spirit, throbbing breast

Why do you make what is natural a crime?
Why do you hide your love?

There's the heart and its yearnings
Then there are the claims of youth
And you have faith in yourself too

Why then do you look at me mortified
Why do you hide your love?

Yes, those who mock us are not human
What do they know of love
Devoid of life are these, stone-hearted men

Aankh aison ki bachaati kyun ho?
Tum muhabbat ko chhupatii kyun ho?

Zulm tumne koi dhaaya to nahiin
Ibn-e Adam ko sataaya to nahiin
Khoon gharibon ka bahaaya to nahiin

Yun pasiine mein nahaii kyun ho?
Tum muhabbat ko chhupatii kyun ho?

Jheinpte to nahiin mandir ke makiin
Jheinpte to nahiin mehrab naqshiin
Jhoot par unki chamaktii hai jabiin

Sach pe tum par sar ko jhukatii kyun ho?
Tum muhabbat ko chhupatii kyun ho?

Parda hai daagh chhupane ke liye
Sharm hai kazb pe chhane ke liye
Ishq ik geet hai gaane ke liye

Iss ko honthon mein dabatii kyun ho?
Tum muhabbat ko chhupatii kyun ho?

Aao ab ghutney ki fursat hii nahiin
Aur bhi kaam hain ulfat hii nahiin
Hai yeh khaami bhi nadaamat hii nahiin

Dar ke chilaman ko utthati kyun ho?
Tum muhabbat ko chhupatii kyun ho?

Why do you avert your eyes from such people?
Why do you hide your love?

You have not been cruel to anyone
You have not troubled any man
You have not shed the blood of the poor

Why then are you bathed in sweat?
Why do you hide your love?

Those who live in temples are not abashed
Those who live in mosques are not mortified
Their foreheads gleam with lies

Why then does truth make you lower your head?
Why do you hide your love?

A veil is meant to hide a stain
Modesty is meant to cover a lie
Love is a song meant to be sung

When then do you stifle it between your lips?
Why do you hide your love?

Come, there is no time for suppressing
There is much to do besides love
It's a failing and not just a regret

Why do you quail at raising the curtain?
Why do you hide your love?

Roosi Aurat ka Naara

Jalaatii hui saikdon gulistan
Chaman par mere phatt padi hai khizaan
Gira kar har ek shaakh se bijliyaan
Uttha kar har ek gul se surkh andhiyaan

Khizaan ko chaman se nikaloongi main
Watan saaf tujhko bacha loongii main

Meri quwwatein raigaan ab nahiin
Hayat-o amal badguman ab nahiin
Mera naam kamzoriyan ab nahiin
Galey mein woh tauq-e giraan ab nahiin

Woh tauq ab galey mein na daloongii main
Watan saaf tujhko bacha loongii main

Meri zindagi markaz-e gham nahiin
Kissi ke qadam par jabiin kham nahiin
Main shola bhi hoon sirf shabnam nahiin
Kissi se kissi tarah bhi kam nahiin

The Call of the Russian Woman

Setting hundreds of rose gardens afire
Autumn has burst upon my garden
Lightning strikes from every branch
Raising red storms from every flower

I will drive out autumn from my garden
I'll save you come what may, my country

My strengths will no longer go waste
Life and work are no longer mistrustful of each other
My name no longer stands for weakness
I no longer have a yoke tied around my neck

I will not put that yoke around my neck again
I'll save you come what may, my country

My life is no longer a hub of sorrows
My forehead is not a resting place for feet
I am fire too, not just a drop of dew
I am not less than anyone in any way

Qadam kaise peechhe hataungii main
Watan saaf tujhko bacha loongii main

Jo ghaafil thhi woh aaj bedaar hai
Jo lori thhi woh aaj lalkar hai
Jo naghma thii woh aaj jhankaar hai
Jo soii thhi woh aaj talwar hai

Galey fatah ko ab laga loongii main
Watan saaf tujhko bacha loongii main

How can I now step back from others
I'll save you come what may, my country

I who was heedless am today mindful
What was once a lullaby is today a rallying cry
What was once a song is today a clamour
What was once a needle is today a sword

I will now embrace victory
I'll save you come what may, my country

Hausla

Tu khursheed hai baadlon mein na chhup
Tu mehtaab hai jagmagana na chhorh

Tu shokhi hai shokhu riaayat na kar
Tu bijli hai bijli jalana na chhorh

Abhi ishq ne haar maani nahiin
Abhi ishq ko aazmaana na chhorh

Courage

You are the sun; don't hide behind the clouds
You are the moon; don't stop shining

You are a coquette; make no concessions in your coquetry
You are the lightning; never stop striking

Love has not conceded defeat yet
Don't stop testing love just yet

Garbhwati

Sun raha hoon yahi besaut karahaein kab se
Hai magar karb hamesha se siwa aaj ki raat
Na tu soya hai no soyega Khuda aaj ki raat

Daii khaamosh kharhi khol rahi hai afyuun
Ghantiyan bajti hain masjid mein dua hoti hai
Neend hii aisi marizon ki dua hotii hai

Pehle bachche mein hua kartii hai takleef aksar
Aakhri ho ke uththa rakha hai toofan iss ne
Kar diya maa ko bhi, dai ko bhi halkaan iss ne

Aise mauluud se duniya ka bhala kya hoga
Kulbulaane se humakne ka hai andaaz juda
Maa se anjaam juda, baap se aaghaaz juda

Kokh se uski bahar haal pur ummeed rahein
Kehte hain garbhwati itni bhi masoom nahiin
Raakshas hoga ke avatar, yeh maloom nahiin

The Pregnant Woman

I have been listening to these silent groans
We have always been afflicted, not just tonight
You have not slept and neither will God sleep tonight

The midwife stands quietly stirring the opiate
Bells ring in temples and prayers are offered in mosques
Sleep is the only medicine for such patients

It's usually the first childbirth that entails such pain
Yet this last one has raised a storm
Tiring out both the mother and the midwife

What good will come to the world from such a birth
There is a difference between spasms and retching agony
The mother is separated from the consequence, the father from
    the genesis

In any case, don't give up on her womb
They say the pregnant woman is not so innocent
No one knows whether she will birth a demon or a god

Iss tazabzub se thakey zehn ko mil jaaye nijaat
Be-asar hai jo dawa kaam dua kar jaaye
Maa se kuchh khauf nahiin, kokh mein bachcha mar jaaye

Aur jarrah yeh kehtein hain ke yeh paap ka phal
Aaj akela nahiin marta hai to maa bhi mar jaaye
Aur yeh kashmakash-e sood-e ziyaan bhi mar jaaye

Yeh bhi mumkin hai ke bachcha jisse hum samjhein hain
Peit khulney pe woh jalta hua mua phorha nikley
Khoon behta hai bahey, zehr to thorha nikley

Kuchh dawa se naa hua hai, naa dua se hoga
Meiz tayyaar karo, garbhwati ko le aao
Peit ko chaak karo, kokh pe nashtar barsao

Kaun sa waqt thha, din kaisey they, haan yaad aaya
Jung uss waqt thhi, ab jung kii tayyari hai
Tab se ab tak wahi manhoos amal jaari hai

Shal huey jaate hain jarraho ke dast-o baazu
Peit mein lagtii hai aari, na chhuri dhansti hai
Meiz par leitii hui garbhwati hanstii hai

This anxiety-ridden mind seeks relief
Prayer might work where medicine fails
There is no danger for the mother, though the baby may die in
    the womb

The surgeons say this is the fruit of sin
If it doesn't die on its own today, let the mother too die
And this conflict between loss and gain also cease

It's also possible that what we assume to be a child
Might turn out to be an erupting boil
Let the blood flow, let the poison drain

Medicines have not helped, nor will prayers
Ready the table for operation, bring the pregnant woman
Cut open her abdomen, rain scalpels upon her womb

What period was it, what was the era, yes, I remember now
There was a war on, even as we prepare for another
The same evil practice continues over the ages

The hands of the surgeons grow numb
Neither saw nor scalpel touches the womb
The pregnant woman lies on the table and laughs

Peetal ke Kangan

Hai yeh peetal ke kangan aur tuu jaan-e bahaar
Woh bhi laya hoon ba-mushkil wai barlail-o nahaar
Tuu magar unn ko pahn kar bhi bahut masruur hai
Kyun na ho khatir mere akhlaas kii manzuur hai

Jab se mere ghar mein tuu aayi haiai muflis nawaaz
Bann gayi hai saari hasti paikar-e soz-o gudaaz
Naujawan dil mein sinaaney ranj ki garhnein lagiin
Aa qabl az waqt rukh par jhurriyan parhnein lagiin
Woh gulabi ankhudiyan woh ras mein duube lab nahiin
Maine jo ghunghat mein dekhe the woh tewar ab nahiin
Matla shaadi pe ghurbat kii udaasi chha gayi
Haif woh ghar jiss mein aa kar khud shama sanwala gayii

Tuu pehn kar unn ko khush rah chhorh jaane de mujhey
Jung ke dankey pe khooni geet gaane de mujhey

Aag barsaoonga aankhon se jidhar jaoonga main
Deo-e zardari ka murda phoonk kar aaoonga main

Brass Bangles

There are these brass bangles and then there's you, the very life
   of spring
I have gone through immense trouble to get them
Yet you are perfectly happy wearing them
And why not since for me they symbolize purity

Ever since you have come to my home, you cherisher of the poor
The universe has come to embody passion and gentleness
Swords of grief stab your youthful heart
And, oh, much before time, wrinkles line your face
Those rose-like eyes and the lips drenched in nectar are gone
The spirit I had seen from behind the veil is gone too
Poverty hangs low over the sky of marriage
Fie the house that dulls the candle upon entering

You be happy wearing them, let me go my way
Let me sing blood-soaked songs to the drumbeats of war

I will rain fire from my eyes wherever I go
I will return after burning the corpse of the monster of capitalism

FILM LYRICS

Waqt Ne Kiya Kya Haseen Sitam*

Waqt ne kiya kya haseen sitam
Tum rahey na tum, hum rahey naa hum

Beqaraar dil iss tarah miley
Jis tarah kabhi hum juda naa thhey
Tum bhi kho gaye, hum bhi kho gaye
Eik raah par chal ke do qadam

Waqt ne kiya . . .

Jaayeinge kahaan, soojhta nahiin
Chal padey magar raasta nahiin
Kyaa talaash hai kuchh pata nahiin
Bun rahein hain dil khwaab dum-ba-dum

Waqt ne kiya . . .

---

* *Kagaz ke Phool*, 1959

What a Beautiful Cruelty
Time Has Inflicted

What a beautiful cruelty Time has inflicted
You have not remained you, I am no longer I

Two restless hearts meet as though
They were never ever apart
You have lost your way, and so have I
Walking a couple of paces down the same road

What a beautiful cruelty Time has inflicted . . .

We know not where we are headed
We have set out though there's no path ahead
We know not what we are looking for
The heart weaves dreams every moment

What a beautiful cruelty Time has inflicted . . .

Zara Sii Aahat Hotii Hai*

Zara sii aahat hotii hai to dil sochta hai
Kahiin yeh woh to nahiin

Chhup ke siine se koi jaise sada deta hai
Shaam se pehle diya dil ka jala deta hai
Hai ussi kii yeh yaad, hai ussi ki yeh ada
Kahiin yeh woh to nahiin
Zara sii aahat hotii hai to dil sochta hai

Shakl phirti hai nigahon mein wahi pyari sii
Meri nas-nas mein machalne lagii hai chingaari sii
Chhu gayii jism mera kiske daaman ki hawa
Kahiin yeh woh to nahiin
Zara sii aahat hotii hai to dil sochta hai

---

* *Haqiqat*, 1964

At the Faintest Footfall . . .

At the faintest footfall my heart wonders
Could it be him?

It is as though someone hides in my breast and calls out
And lights the lamp of my heart well before dusk
It's the way he calls, it is his manner
Could it be him?
At the faintest footfall my heart wonders

That handsome face rising before my eyes
Kindles a spark in every pore of my body
The breeze touching him brushes against me
Could it be him?
At the faintest footfall my heart wonders

Yeh Nayan Darey Darey*

Yeh nayan darey darey
Yeh jaam bharey bharey, zara peene do

Kal kii kis ko khabar
Eik raat ho ke nidar, mujhe jeene do

Raat hasiin, yeh chaand hasiin
Tu sabse hasiin mere dilbar
Aur tujhse hasiin tera pyaar
Tu jaane naa
Yeh nayan darey darey, yeh jaam bharey bharey

Pyaar mein hai jeevan ki khushi
Detii hai khushi kaii gham bhi
Main maan bhi luun kabhi haar
Tu maane naa
Yeh nayan darey darey, yeh jaam bharey bharey

---

* *Kohra*, 1964

122

These Fear-filled Eyes

These fear-filled eyes
These brimful goblets, let me sip from them

Who knows what tomorrow has in store
Let me live without fear just this one night

The night is beautiful, so is the moon
And you, my dearest, are the most beautiful
But even more beautiful is your love
But you don't know . . .
These fear-filled eyes, these brimful goblets

Life's joys lie in love
Some joys come with sorrows too
Even if I ever concede defeat
You never will . . .
These fear-filled eyes, these brimful goblets

Merey Chanda, Mere Nanhe*

Merey chanda, merey nanhe
Tujhe apne seene se kaise lagaoon
Soonii godii mein kaise uthhaoon
Merey chanda, merey nanhe

Chhup gaya ladley aanchal mein
Raat pariyon ka paighaam layii
Kis tarah so gaya tu akela
Kis tarah bin merey neend aayii
Merey chanda, merey nanhe

Terey sapnon mein aa gayii main
Apni majburiyan kya bataoon
Boond bhi tan mein baquii nahiin hai
Bhook teri main kaise mitaoon
Merey chanda, merey nanhe

Aadmi bhi hai, bhagwan bhi hai

---

* *Aakhri Khat*, 1966

My Darling, My Little One

My darling, my little one
How do I hold you close to my heart
How do I pull you into my empty lap
My darling, my little one

You hide in my veil, my pampered one,
As the night brings the message of the fairies
How could you fall asleep alone
How could you sleep without me
My darling, my little one

I will come to you in your dreams
How do I describe my compulsions
Not a drop remains in my body
How do I assuage your hunger
My darling, my little one

There are men, there is God too
And yet you roam helplessly
Who will embrace you

Phir bhi phirta hai tu besahara
Kaun tujh ko galey se lagaaye
Pathharon ka yeh shahr hai saara
Merey chanda, merey nanhe

Door jaana hai nanhe musafir
Raaste mein kahiin thhak naa jaaye
Thhaam kar meri aahon ki dori
Dhoondh le tuhii apna thikaana
Merey chanda, merey nanhe

In this city of stones
My darling, my little one

You have a long way to go, my little traveller
May you not grow weary along the way
Holding on to the thread of my sighs
May you reach your destination
My darling, my little one

Kuchh Dil Ne Kaha*

Kuchh dil ne kaha, kuchh bhi nahiin
Kuchh dil ne suna, kuchh bhi nahiin
Aisi bhi baatein hotii hain

Leta hai dil angrhaaiyan, iss dil ko samjhaiye koi
Armaan naa ankhein khol dey, ruswa na ho jaaye koi
Palkon ki thhandi sej par sapnon ki pariyaan sotii hain
Aisi bhi baatein hotii hain . . . .

Dil ki tasalli ke liye jhuuthi chamak, jhuutha nikhaar
Jeevan to soona hii raha, samjhey sab aayi hai bahaar
Kaliyon se koi poochhta hanstii hain yaa rotii hain
Aisi bhi baatein hotii hain . . . .

* *Anupama*, 1966

The Heart Says Something

The heart says something; no, nothing after all
The heart hears something; no, nothing after all
Such things are known to happen . . .

The restless heart flutters so, someone should tell it to behave
Lest desire open its eyes, disgracing someone in its wake
The fairies of dreams sleep on the cool couches of the eyelids

The heart draws solace from this fake glitter, false elegance
Life remains as barren, while everyone thinks spring has arrived
Who has ever asked the flowers whether they laugh or cry

Dheerey-dheerey Machal
Ai Dil-e Be-qaraar*

Dheerey-dheerey machal ai dil-e be-qaraar, koi aata hai
Yun tarhap ke naa tarhpa mujhey baar-baar, koi aata hai

Usske daaman ki khushbu hawaon mein hai
Usske qadmon ki aahat fizaon mein hai
Mujhko karney de, karney de, solha singhaar
Koi aata hai . . .

Mujhko chhooney lagii usski parchhaiyaan
Dil ke nazdeek bajtii hain shehnaiyaan
Mere sapnon ke aangan mein gaata hai pyaar
Koi aata hai . . .

Rooth ke pehle jii bhar sataoongi main
Jab manaaingey woh maan jaaoongi main
Dil pe rehta hai aisey mein kab ikhtiyaar
Koi aata hai . . .

---

* *Anupama*, 1966

Quieten, Quieten, O Restless Heart

Quieten, quieten, O restless heart, someone is coming
Don't torment me so with every flutter, I hear someone arrive

The breeze carries his fragrance
His footsteps echo all around me
Let me, oh, let me adorn myself
I hear someone arrive . . .

His shadow reaches out to touch me
I hear the shehnai nearby
The melody of love plays in the courtyard of my heart
I hear someone arrive . . .

First I will pretend to be annoyed and trouble him to my heart's
    content
And when he cajoles me I will allow myself to be cajoled
For who has control over one's heart at such times
I hear someone arrive . . .

Abhi Kya Sunogey Suna To Hasogey*

Abhi kya sunogey, suna to hasogey
Ki hai geet adhura, tarana adhura
Jo tum chup rahogey, jo kuchh naa kahogey
Rahega sada yeh fasana adhura

Zamaane se jo maine seekha
Nahiin kuchh bhi woh mere kaam ka
Sikha do jo tum meet merey
Mujhe naghma ik apne naam ka
Sajey subah chehra khiley shaam ka

Qareeb aa ke bhi duur rehna
Tum hii jaano hai iss mein raaz kya
Jo kuchh hai to hai naaz tum par
Karoon apney dil pe main naaz kya
Sada meri kya hai, mera saaz kya

Kisi ka naa ho jis pe saaya

---

* *Satyakam*, 1969

What Will You Hear Now, You Will Laugh If You Do

What will you hear now, you will laugh if you do
For my song is incomplete and so is my melody
If you stay quiet, if you say nothing
This tale will remain incomplete, always

Whatever I have learnt from the world
Is of no use to me whatsoever
But if you were to teach me, my beloved
A song that I can sing for you
It'll brighten the morning and light up the face of the evening

Only you know the mystery in
Keeping your distance while coming so close
If there's any pride to be taken, I take pride in you
There's nothing else I have to be proud of
What price my words, my music

Give me days and nights

Mujhe aisa din aisi raat do
Main manzil to khud dhoondh loongii
Mere haath mein apna haath do
Qadam do qadam tum mera saath do

Untainted by any shadow whatsoever
I will find my destination on my own
Give your hand in mine
And walk beside me a step or two

Maa Hai Mohabbat ka Naam*

Maa hai mohabbat ka naam
Maa ko hazaaron salaam
Kar de fida zindagi
Aaye jo bachchon ke kaam
Maa hai . . .

Hans ke uthhaye gham
Baithey naa haar ke
Paaley zamane ko
Apne ko maar ke
Bhook mitaaye sada
Pyaas bujhaaye sada
Maangey na qimat naa daam
Maa hai . . .

Uske qadam chhoona
Duniya ki shaan hai
Hum ko mila hai jo bhi

---

* *Maa ka Aanchal,* 1970

A Mother Is a Name for Love

A mother is a name for love
A thousand salutations to a mother
She will give up her life gladly
If it were any use for her children
A mother is . . .

She endures sorrows with a laugh
She won't let defeat overcome her
She nurtures the whole world
Denying herself everything
She assuages hunger
And quenches every thirst
Without asking for price or recompense
A mother is . . .

Touching her feet
Brings glory to the world
Whatever we have

Mamta kii daan hai
Baagh lagaati hai Maa
Detii hai khushiyaan tamaam
Maa hai . . .

Chahein bhikaran ho khaali ho haath hii
Maa to rahegii Maa ho koi zaat bhii
Mamta ki zaat taley deep hazaron jaley
Gode mein uss ki paley saare rishi sab imam
Maa hai . . .

Is the legacy of a mother's love
A mother nourishes the garden
Bringing every kind of happiness
A mother is . . .

So what if she is an empty-handed beggar
A mother remains one no matter what her caste
Motherhood shelters a thousand lamps
Her lap nurtures sages and prophets
A mother is . . .

Aaj Socha To Aansu Bhar Aaye*

Aaj socha to aansu bhar aaye
Muddatein ho gayii muskuraaye

Har qadam par udhar murh ke dekha
Unkii mehfil se hum utth to aaye

Reh gayii zindagi dard ban ke
Dard dil mein chhupaiye-chhupaiye

Dil ki nazuk ragein toot tii hain
Yaad itna bhii koi na aaye

---

* *Hanste Zakhm*, 1973

Tears Well Up When I Think of It

Tears well up when I think of it
It's been ages since I smiled

At every step I looked back for a glimpse
Though I turned away from him

Life is now nothing but a pain
A pain I hide in my heart always

The delicate arteries of the heart break
Let no one be remembered so

Betaab Dil Ki Tamanna Yehi Hai*

Betaab dil ki tamanna yehi hai
Tumhey chaaheingey, tumhey puujeingey
Tumhey apna Khuda banaeingey

Soone-soone khwaabon mein jab tak tum naa aaye thhey
Khushiyaan thhii sab auron ki gham bhi saare paraaye thhey
Apne se bhi chhupayii thhi dhadkan apne seene kii
Humko jeena padta thha, khwaahish kab thhi jeene kii
Ab jo aake tumne humey jeena sikha diya hai
Chalo, duniya nai basaingey
Betaab dil ki tamanna yehi hai

Bheegi-bheegi palkon par, sapne kitney sajaey hain
Dil mein jitna andhera thha, utney ujaley aaye hain
Tum bhi humko jagana naa, baahon mein jo so jayein
Jaise khushbu phoolon mein, tum mein yun hii kho jayein
Pal bhar kisi janam mein kabhi chhootey naa haath apna

---

* *Hanste Zakhm*, 1973

142

The Sole Desire of My Restless Heart

The sole desire of my restless heart
Is to love you, worship you
And make you my God

Till you had not entered my desolate dreams
All joys were alien and all sorrows too
I had hidden my heartbeat even from myself
I had to live perforce, though I had no desire to do so
Now that you have come you have taught me to live
Come, let us create a new world
That is the sole desire of restless heart

I have bedecked so many dreams on my moist eyelashes
All the darkness in my heart has given way to light in equal
    measure
You mustn't awaken me if I fall asleep in your arms
Like fragrance in flowers, let me merge with you
Not for a moment ever let go of my hand
Let me embrace you so
That is the sole desire of my restless heart

Tumhe aise galey lagaingey
Betaab dil ki tamanna yehi hai

Vaade bhi hain qasmein bhi beeta waqt ishaaron ka
Kaise-kaise armaa hain, mela jaise bahaaron ka
Saara gulshan de dala kaliyaan aur khilao naa
Hanstey-hanstey ro dein hum itna bhi to hansaao naa
Dil mein tumhii basey ho raha aanchal woh bhi bhar chuka hai
Kahan itni khushi chhupaiyein
Betaab dil ki tamanna yehi hai

Promises need to be made, vows taken, the time for allusions
    is past
Such are the heart's aspirations in this spring-fair
I have given you the entire garden so you can cause more buds
    to bloom
Rein in my happiness lest I break down with joy
Now that you live in my heart what more could I ask for
Where do I hide such happiness
That is the sole desire of my restless heart

Hai Tere Saath Meri Wafa*

Hai tere saath meri wafa, main nahiin to kya
Zinda rahega pyaar mera, main nahiin to kya

Seene mein dard, dil mein tamanna jagaaye ja
Yeh raat jaagne ki hai, shamme jalaaye ja

Tu jashn zindagi ka mana, main nahiin to kya

Tere liye ujaale ki koi kamii nahiin
Sab teri roshni hai, meri roshni nahiin

Koi naya chiragh jala, main nahiin to kya

Kuchh dhadakne ka zikr ho, kuchh dil ki baat ho
Mumkin hai isske baad na din ho naa raat ho

Mere liye naa ashk baha, main nahiin to kya

---

* *Hindustan ki Kasam*, 1973

My Fidelity Will Stay with You

My fidelity will stay with you; so what if I don't
My love will live on, so what if I am not there

Nurture the pain in my breast and hope in my heart
This is a night for wakefulness, keep the candles lit

Celebrate life, so what if I am not there

You will never lack for light
The radiance is all yours, none of it mine

Light a new lamp, so what if I am not there

Let's talk of heartbeats, let's speak of the heart
Hereafter, it's likely there will be neither day nor night

Don't shed any tear for me, so what if I am not there

Har Taraf Ab Yahii Afsaney Hain*

Har taraf ab yahii afsaney hain
Hum terii aankhon ke diwaney hain

Kitni sachchai hai inn aankhon mein
Khotey sikke bhi kharey ho jayein
Tu zara pyaar se dekhey jo idhar
Sookhey jangal bhi harey ho jayein

Baagh ban jaayein jo weerane hain
Har taraf ab yahii afsaney hain

Ik halka saa ishara unn ka
Kabhi dil aur kabhi jaan lootega
Kis tarah pyaas bujhegii uss ki
Kis tarah uska nasha tootega

Jiski qismat mein yeh paimaney hain
Har taraf ab yahii afsaney hain

---

* *Hindustan ki Kasam*, 1973

All Around Me I Hear It Said

All around me I hear it said
I am smitten by your eyes

There is such purity in those eyes
Even spurious coins become genuine
If you were to look at them with love
Even dry forests would become verdant

Wastelands would turn into gardens
All around me I hear it said

The slightest hint from them
Will deprive me of my heart and my life
And the thirst will never be quenched
This headiness will never wear off

Who knows who is destined to drink from these chalices
All around me I hear it said

Neechii nazron mein hai kitna jadu
Ho gaye pal mein kaii khwaab jawaan
Kabhi uthhney, kabhi girney ki ada
Le chali jaane kidhar, jaane kahaan

Raastey pyaar ke anjaane hain
Har taraf ab yahii afsaney hain
Hum terii aankhon ke diwaaney hain

There's such magic in these downcast glances
Many a dream bears fruit in a moment
The way you look up and then lower your gaze
Has taken me who knows where, who knows whither

The ways of love are unknown
All around me I hear it said
I am smitten by your eyes

Koi Yeh Kaise Bataye Ke Woh Tanha Kyun Hai*

Koi ye kaise bataaye ki woh tanhaa kyuun hai
Woh jo apnaa thaa wahii aur kisii kaa kyuun hai
Yahii duniyaa hai to phir aisii yeh duniyaa kyuun hai
Yahii hotaa hai to aakhir yahii hotaa kyuun hai

Ik zaraa haath badhaa de to pakad lein daaman
Unn ke siine mein samaa jaaye hamaarii dhadkan
Itnii qurbat hai to phir faasla itnaa kyuun hai

Dil-e-barbaad se niklaa nahiin ab tak koi
Iss lutey ghar pe diyaa kartaa hai dastak koi
Aas jo tuut gaii phir se bandhaataa kyuun hai

Tum masarrat ka kaho yaa issey gham ka rishtaa
Kahtey hain pyaar kaa rishta hai janam ka rishtaa
Hai janam ka jo yeh rishta to badaltaa kyuun hai

---

* *Arth*, 1982

How Does One Explain . . .

How does one explain why one is lonely
Why is the one who was once mine, now someone else's
If this is what the world is like, why is it so
If this is how things happen, why does it happen so

If you stretch out your hand I could catch your hem
My heartbeat would seep into your breast
If there's such closeness then why this distance

No one ever emerges from the desolation of the heart
Yet someone keeps knocking at this ravaged house
If hope has been dashed, why raise it again

You may call it the bond of joy, or of sorrow
They say the bond of love lasts a lifetime
If it's lifelong, why then does it change so

Jhuki Jhuki Si Nazar . . .*

Jhuki jhuki sii nazar be-qaraar hai ke nahiin
Dabaa dabaa saa sahi dil mein pyaar hai ke nahiin

Tu apne dil ki javaan dhadkanon ko gin ke bataa
Meri tarah tera dil be-qaraar hai ki nahiin

Woh pal ki jis mein mohabbat javaan hotii hai
Uss ek pal ka tujhe intizaar hai ki nahiin

Teri umiid pe thukraa rahaa huun duniyaa ko
Tujhe bhi apne pe yeh eitibaar hai ki nahiin

---

* *Arth*, 1982

This Lowered Gaze

Is this lowered gaze restless, or is it not
No matter how buried, is there love in this heart, or not

Count the youthful beats of your heart and tell me
Is your heart as restless as mine, or not

That moment in which love comes of age
Aren't you too waiting for that one moment, or not

Hopeful of getting you I am throwing away the world
Do you have the same faith in yourself, or not

Tum Itna Jo Muskura Rahey Ho . . .*

Tum itna jo muskura rahey ho
Kya gham hai jis ko chhupa rahey ho

Aankhon mein namin hansin labon par
Kyaa haal hai kyaa dikhaa rahe ho

Ban jaaengey zahr piite piite
Yeh ashk jo piite jaa rahe ho

Jin zakhmon ko vwaqt bhar chalaa hai
Tum kyuun unhein chhedey jaa rahe ho

Rekhaon ka khel hai muqaddar
Rekhaon se maat khaa rahe ho

* *Arth*, 1982

You Are Smiling So Much

You are smiling so much
What's the sorrow you are hiding?

Dampness in your eyes, a smile on your lips
What's your state and what are you showing?

They will turn into poison if you keep drinking
These tears that you are constantly gulping down

The wounds that time has begun to heal
Why do you insist on scraping them

Fate is a game of the lines on your palms
You are being defeated by mere lines

Afterword

My Husband, My Friend: Kaifi Azmi

2002

Each morning a new day dawns and there is birdsong; sometimes clouds gather and raindrops drift into the veranda. Like every other day, our housekeeper Vinod arrives with the tea and puts the tray down in front of me, but the chair facing me is empty. It is not occupied by my Kaifi, who would walk to the garden despite his frail condition and sit in the chair opposite mine, waiting for me to pour out his tea. He would reach out for his cup with trembling hands and look at me in companionship, drinking his tea as though it were ambrosia. These were the most cherished moments of my day. It was under the spell of one such moment that Kaifi composed a poem, 'A Moment':

> Life is nothing but a few moments
> And among those, that one moment
> When two eloquent eyes
> Rise from the cup of tea

And drown in my heart
And doing so, they say:
Don't say anything today
And I won't either
Let's just sit here like this
Holding each other's hand
Cradling the gift of sadness
Nurturing the heat of passions
Who knows in this very moment
In some faraway mountain
The ice might just begin to thaw . . .

Life carries on as usual, Kaifi, but you are nowhere to be found. When you went to the village, I was secure in the knowledge that you would return. I recall a New Year's night when the house was full of revelry. I was rushing around looking after the guests when without warning a little wish awakened in a corner of my heart, 'What if Kaifi were here?' How amazed I was to see you walk through the gate, leaning on your walking-stick. I ran and wrapped my arms around you. '*Arrey wah!* How come you're here? How did you know that your absence was the only thing that was keeping me from feeling happy? How wonderful to have you back. Now that you are here, my New Year will begin.'

How did you turn up suddenly that night? Kaifi, will it never be possible for you to return unannounced and for me to lose myself in your arms. I know this will never be, I shall have to accept the truth that you have gone away to a far-off place from where no one returns. Why does this happen? When will this burden on my heart be lifted? For how long will I have to go on living without you?

Kaifi was not just my husband, he was my friend who never tried to impose his views on me. He never pressured me to do anything I did not like. My wishes and my happiness were always dear to him. In fact, he always tried to help me progress in my work, create a name for myself, be independent and to win people's approval.

In 1947, before we were married and Kaifi was staying at our house in Aurangabad, I had given him a slip of paper on which I had scribbled, 'With you by my side, life will pass by like the morning breeze caressing flowers.' I am amazed how quickly these fifty-five years have passed. My heart remains unfulfilled. I wish Kaifi had stayed with me longer.

In 1977, Kaifi was tackling the stairs of his hotel when he sprained his foot and fell, fracturing his hipbone in three places. His friend, who was with him, had him admitted to the Lucknow Medical College. I was in Bombay; his friend called me, and I took the first possible flight from Bombay to Lucknow. Kaifi's friend Sayyid Muhammad Mehdi was also called from Delhi where he was living at the time. In the hospital I found Kaifi surrounded by doctors. He had tubes coming out of his nose and mouth. His intestines had stopped functioning because of the shock of the fall. I went up to him and whispered in his ear, 'Kaifi, I am here, there is no need to worry.'

After about fifteen to twenty minutes, Dr Goyal, the orthopaedic consultant, said, 'Your presence has given him strength, and slowly but surely, he is improving. If his condition had persisted, we would have had to operate on him.'

Mehdi informed me that the doctors were of the opinion that Kaifi should be kept in Lucknow because it was not advisable to move him to Bombay in his condition. I could do little, but agree. Kaifi was moved into a tiny room with an ensuite bathroom, a kitchen and a small courtyard. Dr Goyal set the bone with skilful precision, but Kaifi's skin was too sensitive to be put in a plaster-cast, and his left leg had to be kept in traction for four months. I stayed with him throughout that time. He could not even turn on his side without assistance, everything had to be done with him lying flat on his back.

In the four months, not one day did I see Kaifi irritable or impatient, but with the dawn of each day he would say, 'Shaukat, thank goodness another day has passed.' At times he would say, 'How will I ever be Sagar's pony again.' Kaifi loved my nephew Irshad's son, Sagar, who was three at the time. To cheer Kaifi up, I hung photographs of Sagar, Baba and Shabana on the wall opposite his bed, so that every morning on waking up he would see his children's photographs.

To this day, I marvel at Kaifi's resilience, because in those four months he never let on that he was in pain; in fact in that condition, he composed a poem from his bed. It was the month of Muharram and there were Shi'a–Sunni riots; dead bodies of young men from both sects were brought to the medical college. His sensitive heart could not bear the pain caused by the news that was brought to him every day by the nurse who was looking after him, and he composed a poem, 'This is not Lucknow'. Shabana, who had taken time out from her film assignments to see her Abba, said in a sad voice, 'Mummy, we can merely see Abba's pain but cannot share it, or reduce it.'

Kaifi was a man of extraordinary will power, and he never despaired. Even a few days before he died, when somebody would ask how he was feeling, he would smile and say, 'First class!' Throughout his life, he was 'first class'. One illness after another assailed him, but he carried on with the task in hand and never accepted defeat. He made it a point to attend every mushaira to which he was invited. In his condition he transformed the future of his tiny village Mijwan, which is thirty-five kilometres from Azamgarh. A tiny village where there was neither a school nor a road, or electricity, or telephone lines. Within fifteen to twenty years he made everything possible, to the extent that he even started a computer class. The most important thing that he did for his village was to have a road constructed connecting it to Phulpur.

Phulpur has a railway station, which at the time was operating on a narrow-gauge railway line with services running between Meerut to Shahganj. Poor farmers travelled to and from Banaras and Azamgarh on that line—the fare was cheap. Phulpur station had been named Khorasan Road station, after some foreigner. One day, the government issued orders for the station to be pulled down, because according to them there was no need for a railway station in Phulpur. Consequently, work began on ripping out the tracks. The poor of the area came to Kaifi with a plea that the station should not be demolished because that would cause them a lot of hardship. Kaifi became anxious, he could not think straight, but arrived directly at the station, and had his wheelchair placed in the middle of the tracks. The stationmaster, worried now, halted work. The young men who were demonstrating against the demolition were being thrashed rather brutally by the police. Among them was Hari Mandir Pandey, a comrade from Kaifi's communist party. This brutality came to an end upon Kaifi's arrival.

Immediately, Kaifi left for Delhi and met Jaffer Sharief who was Minister for Railways at the time. Kaifi said to him, 'Your police have beaten up people from my village so heartlessly that their bodies are drenched in blood. I have brought one of their shirts, I can show it to you if you wish.'

Jaffer Sharief Saheb looked worried and said, 'No, let it be. I'll just give an order that the railway tracks of your village should not be dismantled.' Consequently, taking the order with him, Kaifi returned to the village.

The narrow-gauge line was reinstated, but Kaifi did not remain silent. He demanded a broad-gauge line. By now, a new minister, Ram Vilas Paswan, had taken over. He decided that the narrow-gauge should be converted to a broad-gauge line. As a result, Kaifi and I were invited for the inauguration of the broad-gauge line by Mulayam Singh Yadav. Nevertheless, for Kaifi, this was not enough, because the train did not stop at Phulpur. And, by now, Nitish Kumar had become Minister for Railways. Kaifi made an application to him that trains passing through Phulpur must stop there. Consequently, a superfast train, called Godaan Express—a direct train from Azamgarh to Bombay—stops at Phulpur for three minutes. It operates twice a week—on Sundays and Wednesdays. The villagers have a facility they could not have conceived of in their wildest imagination.

Kaifi's relationship with his children was that of a friend. If ever the children did something wrong, he did not tell them off, but gave his opinion on the matter. Moreover, he loved them beyond measure. Shabana was little, and we were not well off. Mangoes were expensive and were rarely seen at home. One day, Shabana brought two dozen mangoes from her friend Parna's house and told me very happily, 'Mummy, some mangoes came to Parna's house from her village, and her mummy gave me so many.' Shabana loves mangoes. Her words pierced Kaifi's heart, but he remained silent.

After his illness, when the idea of living in his village came to him, all he had left was five bighas of land. After his father and mother left for Pakistan, people from the village had occupied his father's house and land. He was putting up at some relative's. The first thing he did was to hire a truck and go to Malihabad, from where he returned with 300 mango saplings. He planted a mango orchard, and kept a servant, and after five years when they bore fruit, the first thing he did was to bring several hundred mangoes to Bombay for Shabana. That mango orchard is still there, and it's a foregone conclusion that mangoes from there will arrive for Shabana. And this year too, Kaifi's servant brought mangoes for Shabana, but this time Kaifi was not there to witness his daughter's happiness.

At times the words Kaifi uttered could only have come from a sage. For Mijwan's welfare and progress, Kaifi created a welfare society. Its office operated on his land, and he had ceiling fans installed in every room. One night, someone stole all four fans. There was pandemonium in the village, but Kaifi remained silent.

Shabana asked him, 'Aren't you frustrated by what has happened?'

He turned to Shabana and said, '*Bete*, when you are working for change, you should give some leeway to your hope, in the recognition that perhaps this change will not happen in your lifetime, but even so you must carry on with your work.'

Shabana turned to me and said, 'Mummy, hearing Abba, I felt that this is not Abba, but some sage speaking.'

After his son Baba became a cameraman and his first interview was published in a newspaper, Kaifi cut it out, had it framed and hung it on the wall facing his desk. Father and son would sit silently together for hours, but there was exceptional communication between them. Today, Baba says, 'If I can live my life following the path shown to us by Abba, only then will I be able to do justice to his memory.'

Javed Akhtar, who is our son-in-law, has said several times with great pride, 'He is the greatest poet of this age.' Kaifi always addressed his daughter-in-law as, 'Dulhan Pasha', because this is how a daughter-in-law is addressed in Hyderabad. He really enjoyed visiting Baba and Tanvi's home. He wrote his poem,

'*Doosra Banwas*', in my son's house. Speaking about Kaifi in an interview, Tanvi said, 'If you praise Abba, or if he is being given an award, from his expression it seems that it's being given to somebody else and not to him.'

Kaifi was a caring father, an ideal husband, and a man who loved ordinary human beings. His love for his village was like that of someone possessed. He could not bear to hear it criticized, and he loved the Communist Party in a similar manner. He had faith in socialism. He always carried his party membership card in his briefcase, and would often take it out with great pride and say, 'This is my precious capital.' He loved collecting books and Mont Blanc pens. His library has several thousand books, many of which are rare.

People like Kaifi are not born every day. They say people like you do not die, they live forever, but when will I believe this, Kaifi?

Seven Years Later . . .

Shabana has just returned from Mijwan full of excitement at the rapid progress the Mijwan [Welfare Society] has made. Namrata Goyal, the daughter of Jet Airways owners Naresh and Neeta Goyal, has now taken over as President MWS Youth. Namrata has brought on board with her many young people from all over the world on Facebook, Twitter, etc., (I don't even know what that means), but when I see her radiant face bursting with enthusiasm at all the future plans she has for Mijwan, I feel fulfilled.

I remember the last New Year's Eve that I spent with Kaifi in Mijwan. Shabana and Javed were with us. It was a far cry from the boisterous New Year celebrations we used to have in Mumbai. There were just a couple of people from the village gathered around the bonfire in the freezing winter's cold.

I cajoled the shy villagers to sing songs by boisterously taking the lead. Soon the others joined in. Someone sang a folk song off-key much to the amusement of the others. Javed cracked jokes which made everyone scream with delight. The shyest person of the lot suddenly opened up and regaled us with the most amazing mimicry.

Kaifi, who was too ill to join us, sent a message with his nurse Maria to Javed: 'Please sing *"Aye meri Zohra Jabeen"* from the film *Waqt* for my wife from me.' This is a song that Balraj Sahni sings for his wife Achala Sachdev in the film which has become an anthem for older people expressing sentiments of romantic love. Trust Kaifi to always hit the right note, even when seriously ill!

I have visited Mijwan only once after Kaifi passed away. The government was releasing a First Day Cover envelope (postage stamp) on him in Azamgarh and I mustered enough courage to go. It has been six years since, but I find it very difficult to travel now. I only bask in the knowledge that the dream Kaifi had for Mijwan is being carried forward.

I have made peace with my surroundings. I live with Shabana and Javed, but Janki Kutir is still my home. We continue to celebrate Holi there. My life follows a routine. Every morning, I have tea in the drawing room with Shabana and Javed. We read the papers, argue about the headlines. I protest at the rising prices as I stitch my sari blouses with my own hands. At eighty-one, I am still able to work the needle myself.

Shabana keeps teasing me at my abiding passion for saris but I feel happy when her friends exclaim how well dressed I am. I think it is important for senior citizens to be well groomed and look presentable. It enhances your self-esteem and makes you attractive for younger people.

I go for a walk in the evenings where I've made a set of new friends with whom I discuss mundane things. On Sundays, I play cards with Bijon Das Gupta (whom I think of as my own son; he is Baba [Azmi]'s close friend) at Tanvi's house on her behest. I'm addicted to the TV as all old people are. One has to fill in the day somehow. I think older people get so addicted to routine because it is important for them to divide their day into bite-sizes so that the long day doesn't loom ahead interminably.

I am content that I have earned the respect of those around me. It is in part due to their generosity, but it is also in good measure, I think, because I make the effort to be of interest to them. I participate in the love interests of young people who could easily be of my grandchildren's age and am bit of a maverick when it comes to advising them. I believe in love as the single most nurturing of all human relations. People around me are always complaining about the alarming rate of divorce growing among our young people: 'Look at her, just two years into marriage and she has left everything and come back home. Such shame she has brought on us!'

I beg to disagree. Of course divorce is a painful thing for both partners but I don't think that getting divorced is a matter of shame for the parents. I believe parents must keep their doors open for their daughters as they would for their sons. Only then can a daughter have the strength to walk out of a bad marriage.

Today girls are negotiating more space for themselves. A word of caution for them though; when we talk of rights we must not forsake responsibility. Marriage is a process of constant adjustment. Compromise is not a bad word. It is the oil that lubricates any relationship. When we empower our daughters, we must also work to empower our sons so they find the strength to break out of their patriarchal mindset and learn to respect their wives as equal partners. Young women are no longer willing to be treated as appendages to their husbands; they want to be individuals in their own rights. Only then can marriage become the most fruitful of all relationships.

A good marriage makes space for differences, arguments and disagreements because underneath it rests a bedrock of love, trust and true friendship—which is what I shared with Kaifi.

Shaukat Azmi
December 2018

Select Bibliography

Primary Sources

Interviews

Shabana Azmi
Javed Akhtar
Sumantra Ghosal

Secondary Sources

Published Books/Articles (English)

Ali, Ahmed. 1974. 'The Progressive Writers' Movement and Creative Writers in Urdu', in Carlo Coppola (ed.), *Marxist Influences and South Asian Literature*. South Asia Series, Occasional Paper No. 23, Vol. I. East Lansing: Michigan State University.

Ansari, Khizar Humayun. 1990. *The Emergence of Socialist Thought among North Indian Muslims (1917-1947)*. Lahore: Book Traders.

Azmi, Kaifi. 2001. *Selected Poems* (translated by Pavan K. Varma). New Delhi: Viking.

Azmi, Shaukat. 2010. *Kaifi & I* (edited and translated by Nasreen Rehman). New Delhi: Zubaan.

Chandra, Bipan (ed.). 1983. *The Indian Left: Critical Appraisals*. New Delhi: Vikas Publishing House Pvt. Ltd.

Coppola, Carlo (ed.). 1974. *Marxist Influences and South Asian Literature*. East Lansing: Michigan State University.

Jalil, Rakhshanda. 2014. *Liking Progress, Loving Change: A Literary History of the Progressive Writers' Movement in Urdu*. New Delhi: Oxford University Press.

Jalil, Rakhshanda. 2014. *A Rebel and Her Cause: The Life and Work of Dr Rashid Jahan*. New Delhi: Women Unlimited.

Mir, Ali Husain and Raza Mir. 2006. *Anthems of Resistance: A Celebration of Progressive Urdu Poetry*. New Delhi: IndiaInk/Roli.

Pradhan, Sudhi (ed.). 1979. *Marxist Cultural Movements in India: Chronicles and Documents (1936-47)*, Vols. I & II. Calcutta: Distributed by National Book Agency.

Published Books/Articles (Hindi)

Azmi, Kaifi. 2002. *Meri Awaaz Suno*. Delhi: Rajkamal Prakashan.

Published Books/Articles (Urdu)

Azmi, Kaifi. 1994. *Sarmaya*. New Delhi: Mayaar Publications.

Azmi. Kaifi. 2003. *Kaifiyaat: Kulliyat-e Kaifi Azmi*. Delhi: Educational Publishing House.

Azmi, Khalilur Rehman 2002. *Urdu Mein Tarraqui Pasand Adabi Tehreek* (reprint). Aligarh: Educational Book House.

Jafri, Ali Sardar. 1957. *Tarraqui Pasand Adab*. Aligarh: Anjuman-i Tarraqui Urdu.

Jafri, Ali Sardar. 1964. *Lucknow ki Paanch Raatein aur Doosri Yaadein*. Lucknow: Nusrat Publishers.

Mahdi, S.M. 2006. *Chand Tasweerein, Chand Khutoot*. New Delhi: NCPUL.

Zaheer, Sajjad. 1985. *Roshnai*. New Delhi: Seema Publications.